Two Chicago Architects
and Their Clients

Frank Lloyd Wright and
Howard Van Doren Shaw

The MIT Press Cambridge, Massachusetts, and London, England

Two Chicago Architects and Their Clients

Frank Lloyd Wright and Howard Van Doren Shaw

Leonard K. Eaton
with an appendix by Elizabeth M. Douvan

For Charles R. Keller and Luther S. Mansfield

Preface

This book began as an inquiry into the personality characteristics of the early clients of Frank Lloyd Wright. It developed into a study of the larger question of the success and failure of radical architectural innovation or revolution. For some time it appeared to the writer that the early prairie houses of Wright, which in time changed the whole course of domestic architecture in the United States, must have required a rather remarkable type of client. A few years ago I was led to ask the question: What kind of people commissioned dwellings which were as far in advance of their period as these houses?

Now this is a type of question in which architectural historians have not generally been much interested. This lack of interest is the more surprising when we consider that, more than any other artist, the architect is dependent upon the support of his patron. The poet, the painter, and the musician may all compose their works in the hope of future sale. Architecture, however, only begins when a specific person goes to an architect and asks for a particular building. Since it is his money that is involved, the client is undeniably in a position to exert a considerable influence on the design. As I indicate in the first chapter, it would be unthinkable to write the history of Gothic architecture without extensive reference to the personality of Abbot Suger; some of the great patrons of the Renaissance are equally worthy of study, but have, unhappily, not been so thoroughly investigated. On the history of the Modern Movement, and on Wright himself, there have been some excellent books, but none, so far as I know, has treated the role of the client in depth.

In order to attack the problem with all the available weapons, it was obviously desirable to move outside the strictly historical frame of reference. The answers to the question which I had asked clearly involved sociological and psychological considerations, and in dealing with these complex matters I am heavily indebted to Professor Elizabeth M. Douvan of the Psychology Department of the University of Michigan. Professor Douvan has given unstintingly of her time and skill to this project in many ways. In fact, so great are her contributions that it is impossible to enumerate them. She wrote the questionnaire which was our most essential tool, interpreted the data which we obtained, and made creative suggestions at every stage of the endeavor. She has written an appendix, and her thought is evident on every page of the text. It is, in fact, her book as much as mine.

We began, then, with an inquiry into the personalities of the early clients of Frank Lloyd Wright. When that investigation was substantially complete, two points became clear. The first was that we needed a control group of men and women who had chosen to build conventional dwellings at the same time and in approximately the same place. For this purpose the clients of Howard Van Doren Shaw appeared well suited, and so we launched another inquiry. It also became obvious that the material had implications beyond the simple analysis of personality structure. It called for a consideration of the aborted character of the Wrightian revolution. The radical innovations of Abbot Suger were, after all, quite speedily accepted by the society in which he moved. Those of Wright and his clients were rejected by America during the decade of the First World War. We wanted to consider some of the deeper reasons for this rejection.

On this account I have cast the major part of the narrative into a rather dramatic form and used the metaphor of the siege throughout. Wright is seen as the leader of an embattled army attempting to conquer a fortified city. Shaw is viewed as the defending general. If the metaphor seems overly dramatic, I would submit that the story itself has an inherent drama. One has only to read the autobiographies of Sullivan and Wright to realize their feeling that they were involved in a hard-fought battle. Charles Moore's biography of D. H. Burnham is equally clear on the other side. The architects and their clients must therefore be seen as actors on a stage. They are protagonists in a vital struggle, and the stakes are high. At issue is the cultural identity of a great city and an entire region. Will it become a province of the East, or will it achieve true cultural independence? This is, in fact, a question which is still being fought over today. Despite the increasing homogenization of the country, the polarity between the architecture of the Midwest and that of the Eastern seaboard is one of the most basic tensions in American culture. It is probably endemic, and it can be clearly seen in the opposition between the New Chicago School and the work of Paul Rudolph, Louis Kahn, and various other Eastern architects.

A word is in order on the illustrative material. The furnishings with which a couple surrounds themselves are, of course, an important clue to life-style, and hence it is desirable to use vintage photographs wherever possible. With the Wright houses we have generally used the old photographs by Henry Fuermann for the interior. Richard Nickel photographed the exterior of the Greene house for us, and Tom Snodgrass redrew the plans from the original working drawings which were supplied by Mr. and Mrs. Greene. They also graciously consented to allow us to publish the original rendering. Except for the Gilmore plan, which is reprinted through the courtesy of Mrs. Elizabeth Gilmore Holt, other plans are from Henry Russell Hitchcock, *In the Nature of Materials* (Duell, Sloan and Pearce, 1942). Wayne Andrews kindly contributed exterior shots of the Coonley, Boynton, and Heurtley houses. Carrol Eaton took the pictures of the Gilmore House. The 1910 photograph of Wright is reprinted with the permission of the Reinhold Publishing Company. Pictures of Wright's patrons have been supplied by the clients themselves, their sons and daughters, and in the case of Arthur Heurtley, by the Northern Trust Company of Chicago.

With the Shaw houses we have largely depended on the original publications in *The Architectural Record,* except for the Gustavus Swift, Jr., house, which appeared in *The Spur* for July 1, 1918, and the John P. Wilson, Jr., house, which was published in *The Western Architect* in September 1926.

The Prentiss Coonley house has, however, never been published, and we have used exterior and interior photographs taken by Richard Nickel. We think that they show a remarkable continuity of taste. Edward S. Ryerson, Jr., furnished us with a photograph of the oil paintings of his father, and the Chicago Historical Society supplied pictures of Prentiss Coonley, Robert Lamont, and John P. Wilson, Jr. The sons of Clayton Mark provided a portrait of their father. The photograph of Howard Van Doren Shaw came from Mrs. Sylvia Shaw Judson Haskins, and the exterior of his house was taken by Wayne Andrews.

In addition to my debt to Professor Douvan, I have incurred numerous other scholarly obligations in the preparation of this work. Professor Nathan Whitman of the Department of Art read and criticized the section on Renaissance architecture. Professors Carl Condit of Northwestern and James Fitch of Columbia encouraged me at various times, and I am likewise grateful to a number of students who helped out with the fieldwork. While it is impossible to name them all, I would particularly like to mention Peter Forbes, Roger Lang, William Foulks, Christine Simpson, Kenneth Krone, and Ronelle Dubrow. Their interest and enthusiasm meant a great deal. Grants from the Horace H. Rackham Graduate School of the University of Michigan and from the American Council of Learned Societies made possible the employment of two talented research assistants, Arthur Le Gacy and George Mitchell, and their contribution was also substantial. A grant from the American Philosophical Society provided much needed time for reflection and writing. The entire work would, of course, have been impossible without the co-operation of a host of clients and their sons, daughters, and friends who allowed themselves to be interviewed, and to these people I am especially obligated. The section of the work devoted to Howard Van Doren Shaw could not have been done without the co-operation of Shaw's daughters, Mrs. John T. McCutcheon and Mrs. Sylvia Shaw Judson Haskins, and I would like to record here my hope that I have done honor to the memory of their father. Finally I would like to record my profound appreciation to my wife and children for their toleration of my aberrations from normal behavior in the writing of this book. I appreciate their forbearance more than I can say.

Leonard K. Eaton
Ann Arbor, Michigan
September 1968

1 The Problem of
Architectural Innovation in History

The problem of radical shifts in style is one of the knottiest in architectural history. In the history of the West three such shifts have occurred during the last thousand years, and each has signalized the beginning of a new cultural epoch. Although the word is not customarily used in an art-historical context, it will serve our purposes here to call these shifts "revolutions." By revolution the political historian customarily means an upheaval which leaves the power structure of a particular society substantially different from what it was before the event in question took place. The upheaval, of course, may be drastic and thoroughgoing, like the Russian Revolution, or it may be relatively incomplete, like the American Revolution, which was largely organized and carried through by conservatives. In any case the crucial element is the redistribution of power, which puts different groups in control of the essential decision-making apparatus of society.

By architectural revolution, then, we mean a radical shift in style which causes the basic conditions and objectives of building to be substantially different from what they were in the preceding period. Ordinarily, new structural systems and decorative schemes are involved. Sometimes novel building materials are introduced, while in other instances old materials are used in unusual and daring ways. A new sense of space emerges, and with it a new variety of symbolism which is more in keeping with the requirements of the patron, who is himself likely to represent a new power group in society. All of this adds up to a type of building radically different in plan, on the interior and on the exterior, from that which has gone before. Our chief concern here is with the contribution of the patron to the most recent architectural revolution, which took place in Chicago in the nineties and the early twentieth century, but in order to set this upheaval in an appropriate context, it is desirable to study two previous radical shifts in style.

The first of these was from Romanesque to Gothic, and it took place in the Isle-de-France during the decade 1140–1150. The crucial building project was the choir for the abbey church of St. Denis, just outside Paris. Concerning this monument the well-known English architectural historian Nikolaus Pevsner writes, "Whoever designed the choir of St. Denis, one can safely say, invented the Gothic style, although Gothic features had existed before, scattered here and there, and in the centre of France, the provinces around St. Denis, even developed with consistency." [1] While argument still rages about the basic nature of the Gothic, it is reasonable to state that most historians today would agree with Pevsner's identification of St. Denis as the key building of the Gothic revolution. If one compares the choir of St. Denis with that of a major Romanesque church such as St. Sernin at Toulouse (consecrated

3

1096), the nature of the revolution is readily apparent. The dissolution of the wall by means of an entirely new structural system has created a new sense of space. A new intellectual and artistic spirit is at hand.

Precisely because the new choir at St. Denis was such a revolutionary building, we know more about its great sponsor, Abbot Suger, than about any of the other great Gothic patrons of the twelfth and thirteenth centuries. Erwin Panofsky has demonstrated in masterly fashion the manner in which Suger's own personality and beliefs affected the design, and Otto Von Simson has stressed the need of the French monarchy, with which Suger was closely associated, for a new kind of building which could symbolize its growing power. Both scholars have dealt with the importance of Suger's metaphysic of light for the development of the Gothic style. In short, enough material has been uncovered so that we are justified in claiming that one man, Abbot Suger, came close to bringing about an architectural revolution.

The second radical shift in style occurred in Florence during the third and fourth decades of the fifteenth century, and it was, of course, the change from Gothic to Renaissance. Because the Florentine merchants have not yet been sufficiently studied as patrons of architecture, it is not so easy to fix responsibility for the new movement as it is with Suger. So far as is known, none of them wrote in the same way about their attitudes toward the building projects with which they were involved as did Suger. The picture is further complicated by the split between ecclesiastical and secular design which began to emerge at about this time. For their family church, San Lorenzo, the Medici, who were the greatest patrons of the age, employed Filippo Brunelleschi, the most progressive architect of the city. Thereby they obtained a building which broke radically with the tradition of the Florentine church. A comparison of the nave of San Lorenzo (designed 1418, built 1421–1460) with that of the Gothic church of Santa Croce will reveal the sharpness of the break. New forms, new proportions, and a new kind of space inaugurate a new age.

For their family palace, on the other hand, Cosimo de Medici, who was the chief of the clan, rejected the design of Brunelleschi, supposedly on the grounds that it would have been too expensive to build and would have aroused too much jealousy among the other merchant princes of the city. "Envy," he supposedly remarked, "is a plant one should never water." In any event, the Medici employed Brunelleschi's more malleable follower Michelozzo to build their palace, which was a much more traditional structure. In the area of palace architecture the real innovators were apparently the Rucellai family and their architect, the famous Leon Battista Alberti. In their palace

(1440–1451) classical elements, in this case pilasters, are used for the first time to articulate a bearing wall. These elements are also employed to produce new proportions and to suggest a modular system of design. Hence this building became the ancestor of a whole line of important structures, running down through the grand baroque palaces of the seventeenth and eighteenth centuries. A comparison of the Medici and Rucellai palaces suggests that in this area the taste of the Medici was somewhat conservative, as Frederick Antal has shown it was in sculpture and painting.

These examples are introduced here to stress the point that we are concerned with *radical* shifts in style. The ordinary course of architectural development in most periods is much more sedate. In Georgian England, to cite one final case for contrast, there appears to be a relatively steady and unwavering development from Lord Burlington in the early eighteenth century to the great Regency architect John Nash. Kent, Gibbs, Chambers, and the Adam brothers all worked with more or less the same artistic vocabulary and the same type of structure. While many of their buildings are of exceptional quality architecturally, none are revolutionary in the sense that we are using the word here.

The third great architectural revolution in Western culture is much closer to us. It occurred in Chicago during the years 1890–1913, and there are still people alive who were associated with it. The chief actor in the drama was, of course, Frank Lloyd Wright, and it is his clients who will concern us. So far it appears that in order to have a revolutionary architecture you must have an unusual type of client. In the twelfth century Abbot Suger was unquestionably a new kind of actor on the European stage. He was, in fact, the first of the great royal administrators who were to play a major part in the affairs of Western Europe. He was also, and perhaps this is more important, a poor boy who made good on a grand scale. With his customary felicity Erwin Panofsky has illuminated Suger's character:

To understand this psychological phenomenon, we have to remember two things about Suger that again place him in diametrical contrast to the highborn convert, St. Bernard. First, Suger entered the monastery, not as a novice devoting himself to monastic life of his own free will, or at least with the comprehension of a relatively mature intelligence, but as an oblate dedicated to Saint Denis when a boy of nine or ten. Second, Suger, the schoolmate of young noblemen and princes of the blood, was born—no one knows where—of very poor and very lowly parents.

Many a boy would have developed into a shy or bitter person under such circumstances. The future Abbot's extraordinary vitality resorted to what is known as overcompensation. Instead of either clinging to or drastically breaking away from his natural relatives, Suger kept them at a friendly distance and, later on made them participate in a small way in the life of the Abbey. Instead of either concealing or resenting his humble birth, Suger almost gloried in it, though only to glory all the more in his adoption by St. Denis. "For who am I, or what is my father's house?" he exclaims with the young David. And his literary works as well as his official documents fairly bristle with such phrases as: "I, insufficient with regard to family as well as knowledge;" or: "I, who succeeded to the administration of this church against the prospects of merit, character and family," or (in the words of Hannah, mother of Samuel): "I, the beggar, whom the strong hand of the Lord has lifted up from the dunghill." But the strong hand of the Lord had operated through the Abbey of St. Denis. In taking him away from his natural parents, he had given to Suger another "mother," an expression persistently recurring in his writings, who had made him what he was. It was the Abbey of St. Denis which had "cherished and exalted him;" which had "most tenderly fostered him from mother's milk to old age;" which "with maternal affections had suckled him as a child, had held him upright as a stumbling youth, had mightily strengthened him as a mature man and had solemnly set him among the princes of the Church and the realm."

Thus Suger, conceiving of himself as the adopted child of St. Denis, came to divert to the Abbey the whole amount of energy, acumen and ambition nature had bestowed upon him. Completely fusing his personal aspirations with the interests of the mother church, he may be said to have gratified his ego by renouncing his identity: he expanded himself until he had become identical with the Abbey.[2]

Finally, Panofsky comments on the psychological significance of Suger's frail physique, linking him in this respect with certain other "great little men"—that is, Napoleon, Mozart, Erasmus, and General Montgomery. A combination of pluck and the will to fellowship, he argues, characterized them all.

While we have no such subtle psychological analysis of Cosimo de Medici, we do know a good deal about him and about his almost equally interesting contemporary Giovanni Rucellai. At the outset it is clear that Cosimo's attitude toward the arts was quite different from that of Suger, if not diametrically opposite. Born (1389) to wealth and power, he viewed enjoyment and patronage of the arts as a perquisite and responsibility of his position. Coming to maturity in the exciting decade 1420–1430, he seems genuinely to have enjoyed his contacts with artists, particularly Filippo Brunelleschi, and after the death of Cosimo's father in 1429, the two were frequently in touch about the building of the family church, San Lorenzo. In fact, it became a veritable passion with him. "It was the first thing that he built," says Vasari, "and he took such delight in it that up to the time of his death he was always erecting something there. Cosimo prosecuted this work with more ardour, and while one thing was under deliberation had another one completed. Having taken up this work as a pastime, he was almost continuously at it."[3]

How did it happen, then, that Cosimo rejected Brunelleschi's design when he decided to build a new palace for himself (which would also be a headquarters for the family business)

6

about 1440? Curt Gutkind, his biographer, suggests that the explanation may lie in the character of the commission itself. Cosimo needed not only a new and roomier house, which would be in keeping with his position as the town's first citizen, but also new storerooms, offices, and countinghouses, which could handle the firm's increasing commercial and industrial activities. "The new palazzo," he writes, "was to be built in the first place for a definite purpose—a utilitarian purpose.[4] He does not believe that Cosimo was influenced by a desire for "Renaissance seigneurial dignity" or "princely magnificence." Simple economic objects and necessities were uppermost in his mind. An additional point in favor of this contention is that Cosimo himself was, by all accounts, a reticent and unassuming man. It was, after all, not he but his grandson who was known as "the magnificent."

In the light of this information, Cosimo's behavior becomes understandable. His first impulse was to give the job to Brunelleschi, whom he liked and who had served him well at San Lorenzo. When he saw Brunelleschi's design, however, he realized that it was not in keeping with his true requirements, and gave the job to the less talented but more utilitarian Michelozzo. This is a perfectly understandable decision. Gutkind therefore suggests that Cosimo followed his own harmonious and purposeful taste in the construction of his palace and that the original simple, compact, well-ordered building, much smaller than the present structure, is very much in his spirit. Finally, he indicates that in Cosimo's mind the real significance of the tall Rustica, with its huge, dimly lighted, vaulted cellars, which may have developed from the fortresslike ground-floor apartments of the thirteenth century, lay in its suitability as storerooms for bales of cloth and silk.

With Cosimo's example in mind, the behavior of Giovanni Rucellai in commissioning Leon Battista Alberti to design his palace is all the more striking. Rucellai (1403–1481) came from the old Florentine mercantile patriciate and amassed a large fortune in the wool trade. Because of his connections with the Strozzi family, he was at first distrusted by the Medici, but over the course of time redeemed himself by his circumspect conduct toward them. In 1461 Cosimo gave Nannina, daughter of his son Piero, to Giovanni's son Bernardo in marriage, and the two great families were allied. Two years later Giovanni Rucellai was elected prior, and in 1475 he became gonfalonier of justice for the republic under the regime of Lorenzo the Magnificent. In his memoirs, which were published by the Warburg Institute in 1960, he exhibits an enthusiasm for building comparable with that of Cosimo, but never mentions his reasons for employing Leon Battista Alberti, the most significant and most progressive architect of the mid-quattrocento. Since the Rucellai palace was Alberti's first Florentine commission, a word about his background is in order.

An illegitimate son of a good Florentine family, Alberti was born in 1404 in Genoa, where his parents had been exiled. He received a humanistic education at Padua and the University of Bologna, studied mathematics, literature, and philosophy, and in general endeavored to make himself into the ideal "universal Renaissance man." In 1428 the Signoria revoked the ban against his family, and, says Bruno Zevi, "Alberti discovered architecture, but the encounter was brief in duration."[5] During the next few years he became a papal civil servant, traveled widely in Europe, and also resided in Rome from 1431 to 1434. While in that city he studied the ancient monuments "with scrupulous diligence," measuring them with instruments of his own devising. In 1434 a political upheaval forced the Curia to flee the city, and Alberti spent most of the next three years in Florence, where he was immediately accepted in humanistic circles. Probably he knew the great Brunelleschi, and evidently he admired him, for he dedicated his 1435 treatise on painting to this key figure of the Renaissance. In 1438 he attended the Council of Ferrara, and it was from Lionello d'Este of the great Ferrara family that he first received recognition as a man competent in the arts and probably in architecture. In 1443 he was recalled to Ferrara to judge the competition for the monument to Nicholas III d'Este. Zevi states that Lionello probably accepted his suggestions for the pedestal, the so-called Arco del Cavallo, and the bell tower of the cathedral. After his return to Rome he was apparently consulted about the condition of the tottering basilica of St. Peter's in 1447 and seems to have directed the restoration of certain churches including San Stefano Rotondo, Santa Prassede, and Santa Maria Maggiore. This was his first practical experience in building.

In view of his lack of such experience it may seem surprising that Giovanni Rucellai engaged Leon Battista Alberti to design his palace. In point of fact, it was not a strange decision at all. Alberti was already known as a first-class theoretical mind and one of the leading mathematicians of the age. He was the first to call himself "geometra" — that is, one who proposed to bring mathematics to the solution of all sorts of scientific and artistic questions. The Renaissance believed that men with this kind of generalized intelligence could handle almost any kind of problem, and it was therefore not at all surprising that Rucellai, who was well acquainted with humanist thought, should have turned to him. Moreover, his memoirs (the narrative entitled *Zibaldone*) revealed him to have been primarily concerned with his responsibility to his family and to his parish, not with his own personal achievements. "The buildings he commissioned," says Gertrude Bing, "all situated within the narrow confines of the Rucellai parish, were in his eyes family concerns; and the decoration on the facade of his Palazzo reflects preoccupations found again in the *Zibaldone*." [6] According to Aby Warburg, the Rucellai coat of arms reflects the thinking of Giovanni's favorite philosopher, Marsilio Ficino, and the family's close alliance with the Medici. We would suggest, then, that precisely because this facade was such an extremely personal statement, it could become a striking bit of architectural progressivism. The Rucellai were not the first citizens of Florence, and their architecture reflected their position just below the very top brackets.

Finally, it should be noted that Alberti became a family architect for the Rucellai to a much greater extent than did Brunelleschi for the Medici. He not only designed the palace, but built a little loggia opposite it, added a chapel to the family church at San Pancrazio, and redesigned the facade of Santa Maria Novella as a gift from the family to the city. In contrast, Brunelleschi built nothing for the Medici after the completion of San Lorenzo, though it seems highly probable that a follower did the graceful monastery church and cloister at the Badia di Fiesole during the years 1456–1466. Michelozzo, a much more conservative artistic personality, was apparently Cosimo's favorite architect. Besides the palace on Via Larga, now Via Cavour, Michelozzo at Cosimo's request made extensive additions to the old church of San Marco, also designed the first public library in Italy, the Marciana, and finally, built the famous villa at Careggi where his patron died. Except for the villa, all of this was done while Brunelleschi was in full command of his powers.

In Renaissance Florence, then, we have a situation where the leading family of the city employs the town's most progressive architect for their single most important building project, but prefers a less daring designer for their private residences and less important undertakings. Another great family takes the lead in sponsoring the new architecture in the secular area. While the origins of these decisions cannot be analyzed too closely, it would appear that personal reticence and fear of conspicuous display were major elements in Cosimo's thinking. Giovanni Rucellai had no such motivations, and his various building projects reveal a more progressive spirit. Much the same comment can be made about his art collection. He owned pictures by Castagno, Uccello, and Antonio Pollaiuolo, and sculpture by Verrochio. In the climate of fifteenth-century Florence all may be considered "progressive" artists. Recalling that Suger was a parvenu, we may suggest that in these two instances advanced architectural design is a natural province for the secondary strata of the aristocracy.

9

In broader terms we may observe that Suger and his unknown architect, together with Rucellai and Alberti, were flinging down a challenge to the established architectural canons of taste in their respective worlds. These challenges were clearly understood by their contemporaries, and it would be a mistake to believe that the innovations were accepted all at once. While the Gothic did in time become the preferred style of the Capetian monarchy, a number of important clerical leaders, especially among the monastic orders, were reluctant to accept it. In the outlying lands of Europe, such as Spain, excellent Romanesque work was done well into the fourteenth century. Similarly, not all the Florentine merchants welcomed the innovations which we have discussed. The Strozzi Palace (begun 1489) is an extremely reactionary building. In order to tell the story completely we should have to take up the opposition to the revolutionaries. Conservatives, however, often tend to be inarticulate, and commentaries on architectural taste in twelfth-century France and fifteenth-century Italy are, in any event, scarce. Nonetheless, it is clear that in the long run the new styles did appeal to influential groups in society. Within two generations after the death of Suger in 1154, the Gothic was the official architecture of the French monarchy, which was the strongest political force in Western Europe, and by the late fifteenth century the architectural impulse begun in the work of Brunelleschi and Alberti had flowered in the High Renaissance at Rome.

The challenge to established architectural standards thrown down by Frank Lloyd Wright and his contemporaries was as radical as that of Suger's master builder or of Brunelleschi and Alberti. Did the clients who sponsored it resemble in any way Abbot Suger, Cosimo de Medici, or Giovanni Rucellai? This is the question to which we must address ourselves. It is our good fortune that we are still close enough in time to the nineties and the first decade of this century so that it is possible to investigate in some detail the sort of person who sponsored the third (or Wrightian) architectural revolution. In terming it "Wrightian" we would like to make it very clear that Mr. Wright was not the only revolutionary. Louis Sullivan was very definitely the father of this particular upheaval, and various other architects, notably Walter Burley Griffin, Purcell and Elmslie, Hugh Drummond, and George Maher, also contributed to it. The landscape architect Jens Jensen and the poets Carl Sandburg and Vachel Lindsay were in full sympathy with its goals and were, in fact, also revolutionary in their respective fields. Wright, however, was acknowledged as its leader by his own contemporaries, and was also the artist who pushed it to the greatest extremes. If we may make an analogy to the French Revolution, Sullivan was its Danton, Wright was its Robespierre, and Daniel Burnham and Howard Van Doren Shaw ultimately became the leaders of the men of Thermidor. It is therefore more logical to study Wright's clients than those of any other architect.

Of what did the architectural revolution consist? Many books have been written to answer this question, and it is not our purpose to deal with it here. Briefly, we may say that its most distinctive feature was the freeing up and enlivening of interior space. There were, indeed, many other achievements, but they were all subordinate to this objective. As usual Nikolaus Pevsner has put the matter nicely. He writes:

The first private houses in which the new, original style of the 20th century can be recognized are Frank Lloyd Wright's (born 1869), built in the neighborhood of Chicago. [It has now been demonstrated that the correct birth date was 1867.] They have the freely spreading ground plans, the interweaving of exteriors and interiors by means of terraces and cantilevered roofs, the opening up of one room into another, the predominant horizontals, the long window bands that are familiar in today's houses.[7]

From the point of view of the client, all this meant that he would get a house which *looked* different from the customary dwelling of the time and which was built around behavior patterns that were also different. These variations from the norm were all recognized. Mr. Frederick C. Robie, one of the best known of Wright's clients, remarked, "I did a little traveling around, and ran across a constant fillip: 'I know what you want, one of those damn Wright houses.'"[8] It evidently took a certain degree of courage to build a Wright house.

The career of Frank Lloyd Wright is filled with paradoxes, and one of them is indicated in the remark by Mr. Robie quoted just previously: that he developed a truly revolutionary architecture in a milieu which was seemingly hostile to art. The early years of his practice are so closely identified with Oak Park that it is well to examine that interesting community rather closely. In a sense his residence there was an accident. In 1887 he and his mother took rooms with the Reverend Augusta Chapin, a Unitarian minister then serving as a pastor to the Unitarian Congregation in Oak Park. Miss Chapin, an old friend, lived in a house which Grant Manson, Wright's biographer, described as "a gingerbread villa only a few steps from the present noisy traffic on Lake Street, the main thoroughfare."[9]

The Wrights had been understandably dissatisfied with the boardinghouse near All Souls Church on the south side of Chicago where they were living, and the pleasant atmosphere of Oak Park, a small, leafy suburb at the western edge of the city, reminded them of their Wisconsin home. At about this same time Wright fell in love with Catherine Tobin, an attractive girl whom he met in the congregation at All Souls. In 1889 he asked her to marry him, and not surprisingly soon thereafter bought a lot in a new Oak Park subdivision. In the fall of 1889 with the assistance of a loan from Adler and Sullivan, he began building his own house. In the next two decades he was to build more than twenty houses and a major church for the suburb where he had settled. Even today the casual visitor to Oak Park will be surprised at the number of obvious builder's houses which employ Wright's details. Evidently his impact on the physical face of the town was substantial.

What sort of place was Oak Park? Since this community and its surrounding suburbs were the true setting of the Wrightian revolution, it is proper to pay some attention to the milieu. It was certainly a milieu which bore little resemblance to the France of Abbot Suger. That society was dominated by an aristocracy based on military skill and the hereditary possession of land. Oak Park was perhaps somewhat closer to the Florence of Cosimo de Medici, which was controlled by great families that had accumulated wealth in commerce and finance. It was a residential suburb whose citizens were primarily Chicago businessmen and their families. These men were company executives, manufacturers, bankers, and professional people who commuted to the Loop each day via the Chicago and North Western Railroad. For several years Wright himself found it necessary to maintain a downtown office for conversations with prospective clients, though his main headquarters was the combination house and studio which he built for himself and his family on Forest Avenue.

In 1900 Oak Park was on the verge of a period of extraordinary growth. The population was approximately nine thousand, nearly twice what it had been in 1890; it was to double again in the next decade. During this decade 1900–1910 the community went far to solve the traditional urban problems of street paving and lighting, sewage disposal, and fire and police protection. It was especially notable for its excellent educational system; graduates of the Oak Park High School generally found little difficulty in gaining admission to Eastern colleges. It had a good library and a phenomenal number of organizations devoted to various types of cultural uplift. Music occupied an important place in the community. There were a number of orchestral and vocal groups active around the turn of the century. Oak Park even opened its own opera house in 1902, with a seating capacity of fifteen hundred and employing forty professional performers. Local talent supplied the chorus. This endeavor was, however, too ambitious to be supported, and the opera company dissolved within a few years. Thereafter the Warrington Opera House was used by stock companies and amateur theatricals.

Because of the importance of one of Oak Park's sons, a good

deal has been written about the town, and we can make certain further generalizations concerning its character. Ernest Hemingway was born in Oak Park on July 21, 1899, to Dr. and Mrs. Clarence E. Hemingway, two prominent citizens of the town. Several of his critics and biographers have commented on the rather special aspects of his early environment. In the *Apprenticeship of Ernest Hemingway,* Charles A. Fenton writes, "The community was more than respectable. It was respectable and prosperous. It was also Protestant and middle class. It exulted in all these characteristics. For Oak Park there was nothing ludicrous in its qualities." [10] Those who were lucky enough to reside there were very clear that they lived in Oak Park, *not* in Chicago. It resisted incorporation into the city (it still does), and its affairs had a strong New England town-meeting flavor. Other aspects of Oak Park also had a puritanical quality. There were a number of delicate gradations in the social hierarchy, even though most citizens apparently thought that there was no "other side of the tracks" in their town. "The center of social life, even for the most sophisticated, was the school and the family church," [11] says Fenton perceptively, and adds that Oak Parkers usually defined the town as "where the saloons end and the churches begin." It was, of course, dry. In sum, it would be hard to find a community which was a better example of the Midwestern Victorian era of the nineties.

Hemingway's family fitted neatly into this milieu. Concerning their parents his brother has written,

But as was common in the vast middle class of the Middle West, they believed themselves to be members of the upper class. They prided themselves on their interest in church missionary work and the fine arts. They aided all sorts of uplift movements, ranging from the establishment of nature study groups — Father founded the local branch of the Agassiz Society — to Protestant missionary societies dedicated to spreading the Word all over the world. [12]

Hemingway's father was an avid hunter and fisherman, and as is well known, inculcated a taste for these sports in his son. His mother, on the other hand, was essentially of an artistic temperament. She had a fine voice, studied in New York, and was always rankled by the fact that her marriage forced her to give up a musical career. Leicester Hemingway speaks of her as a "cultural arbiter," and in 1904 when funds became available which enabled the family to build a house, it was she who designed it. The new dwelling had fifteen rooms, "including a thirty-by-thirty music room two stories high with a balcony — very impractical as far as heating went, but fine for recitals and concerts. Later it was used for painting exhibitions." [13] Here young Ernest had to practice the cello.

Enough has been written about the Hemingway family so that we can speak of its conflicts and problems with some accuracy. While it would be unfair to generalize from this one

13

example to the rest of Oak Park, analysis of its problems may help to illuminate a few of the basic situations which probably occurred with some frequency elsewhere in the town. It will, at any rate, indicate the level of complexity with which we are dealing and will certainly help to overcome what might be called the *Ah, Wilderness* stereotype: the notion that pre-World War I America was filled with large white houses containing families which got along together easily. Father ruled over his large brood as a good-natured despot, and Mother was essentially a balance wheel. Brothers and sisters teased each other a good deal, but the ugly words "sibling rivalry" were unknown. Divorce was unheard of, and the family was altogether a more viable unit than it is today. This stereotype, which can be seen in any number of movies, novels, and plays, scarcely describes the actual conditions in the Hemingway family.

Briefly stated, the family was racked by tension between an artistic mother and a Spartan father. On the surface the Hemingways resembled the happy group of *Ah, Wilderness,* but in fact, life was filled with emotional crises. Leicester Hemingway has remarked that whenever these occurred, their mother would rush to her room, draw the shades, and declare that she had a sick headache. Despite the fact that he was a considerable success at the difficult Oak Park High School (a football player and swimmer, track manager, member of the school orchestra, and an editor of the student paper), Ernest Hemingway had a stormy adolescence.

He recalled some of his feelings about his parents in a semi-autobiographical short story, "Soldier's Home," which suggests his negative reactions to the exaggerated piety of his mother and to his parents' demand that he go out and get a job after his return from the First World War. They were, in fact, completely unsympathetic to his literary ambitions. When his first book (*In Our Time*) was published, his father returned all of the copies which the publisher had sent to him because he thought the stories were obscene. It would be hard to find a better symbol of parental rejection. Charles Fenton quite rightly remarks that "a number of unpleasant things happened to Hemingway in Oak Park." [14] It is no wonder that in 1952 he said that he had a wonderful novel to write about Oak Park but would never do so for fear of hurting living people.

This, then, was the milieu in which Frank Lloyd Wright built his practice—prosperous, middle-class, in religion strongly Protestant, in ethnic structure white and Anglo-Saxon, and in family character possessing many more conflicts than the casual observer might think. All of these characteristics Oak Park shared with the other suburbs where Wright built his houses in fair numbers—Riverside, River Forest, Hinsdale, LaGrange, Geneva, and Glencoe. In the small towns outside

14

the Chicago area, such as Kankakee, Illinois, and Springfield, Ohio, they were, if anything, exaggerated. We may think of all these places as being filled with people who in varying ways resembled the Hemingways. That Suger, a prince of the Church with a strategic political position, should sponsor a revolutionary architecture is understandable. That Cosimo de Medici and Giovanni Rucellai, members of an established and cultivated mercantile patriciate, should act similarly is also comprehensible. But that a revolutionary architecture should blossom in the Chicago suburbs of 1890–1913 is, at first glance, wildly improbable. The question now before us is: How did it happen?

1 Footnotes

[1] Nikolaus Pevsner, *An Outline of European Architecture* (New York, 1948), p. 31.

[2] *Abbot Suger on the Abbey Church of St. Denis and its Art Treasures,* ed., annot., and trans. by Erwin Panofsky (Princeton, 1946), pp. 30–31.

[3] Giorgio Vasari, *Lives of the Most Eminent Painters, Sculptors, and Architects,* trans. Gaston Du C. De Vere (London, 1912–1914), vol. II, p. 225.

[4] Curt Gutkind, *Cosimo de Medici Pater Patriae* (Oxford, 1958), p. 220.

[5] Bruno Zevi, "Alberti," article in *McGraw-Hill Encyclopedia of World Art* (New York, 1959), p. 187.

[6] Gertrude Bing, introductory note to *Giovanni Rucellai ed il Suo Zibaldone* (the Warburg Institute, London, 1960), p. IX.

[7] Pevsner, *Outline,* p. 210.

[8] "Mr. Robie Knew What he Wanted." *Architectural Forum* (CIX, 1958), p. 127.

[9] Grant Manson, *Frank Lloyd Wright to 1910: The First Golden Age* (New York, 1958), p. 42.

[10] Charles A. Fenton, *The Apprenticeship of Ernest Hemingway* (New York, 1954), p. 2.

[11] *Ibid.,* p. 4.

[12] Leicester Hemingway, *My Brother Ernest Hemingway* (Cleveland, 1962), p. 20.

[13] *Ibid.,* p. 26.

[14] Fenton, *Apprenticeship,* p. 2.

15

16
1. Nave of St.
Sernin, Toulouse.
Photo: Giraudon

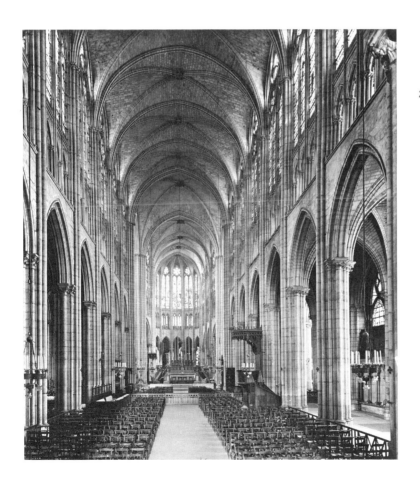

17

2. Nave of Abbey
Church of St.
Denis. Photo:
Giraudon

3. Nave of Church
of Santa Croce,
Florence. Photo:
Alinari

18

4. Nave of Church
of San Lorenzo,
Florence. Photo:
Alinari
19

20
5. Medici Palace,
Florence. Photo:
Alinari

21

6. Rucellai Palace,
Florence. Photo:
Alinari

2 Frank Lloyd Wright
and the Siege of the City

In Chicago and its suburbs during the years 1893–1913 Frank Lloyd Wright found a sufficient number of radical clients to let him develop a revolutionary architecture. It was an architecture so far in advance of its time that in certain respects contemporary architects are still trying to catch up with it. While a handful of public buildings such as Unity Temple and the Larkin Building in Buffalo are undeniably important, many of Wright's most significant innovations were made in the area of domestic architecture. This was the field in which he was to do a large part of his work for the rest of his days and in which he was to make his single greatest contribution. It is therefore worthwhile to inquire here about the exact nature of the Wrightian revolution. Because Wright was an embattled personality who saw himself as the leader of a crusade, we have called this revolution the siege of the city.

An immense amount has been written about the problem. In our view we can do no better than to quote Wright himself. Years after the Oak Park Period, he said that his main motives and indications were:

First—

To reduce the number of necessary parts of the house and the separate rooms to a minimum, and make all come together as enclosed space—so divided that light, air and vista permeated the whole with a sense of unity.

25
1. Frank Lloyd Wright, age 37, courtesy of Reinhold Publishing Co.

Second—
To associate the building as a whole with its site by extension and emphasis of the planes parallel to the ground, but keeping the floors off the best part of the site, thus leaving that better part for use in connection with the life of the house. Extended level planes were found useful in this connection.

Third—
To eliminate the room as a box and the house as another by making all walls enclosing screens—the ceilings and floors and enclosing screens to flow into each other as one large enclosure of space, with minor subdivisions only. Make all house proportions more liberally human, with less wasted space in structure, and structure more appropriate to material, and so the whole more livable. Liberal is the best word. Extended straight lines or streamlines were useful in this.

Fourth—
To get the unwholesome basement up out of the ground, entirely above it, as a low pedestal for the living portion of the home, making the foundation itself visible as a low masonry platform on which the building should stand.

Fifth—
To harmonize all necessary openings to "outside" or to "inside" with good human proportion and make them occur naturally—singly or as a series in the scheme of the whole building. Usually they appeared as "light-screens" instead of walls, because all the "architecture" of the house was chiefly the way these openings came in such walls as were grouped about the rooms as enclosing screens. The room as such was now the essential architectural expression and there were to be no holes cut in walls as holes are cut in a box, be-

2. Wright house, courtesy of Henry-Russell Hitchcock

cause this was not in keeping with the ideal of "plastic." Cutting holes was violent.

Sixth—

To eliminate combinations of different materials in favor of mono-material so far as possible; to use no ornament that did not come out of the nature of materials to make the whole building clearer and more expressive as a place to live in, and give the conception of the building appropriate revealing emphasis. Geometrical or straight lines were natural to the machinery at work in the building trades then, so the interiors took on this character naturally.

Seventh—

To incorporate all heating, lighting, plumbing so that these systems became constituent parts of the building itself. These service features became architectural and in this attempt the deal of an organic architecture was at work.

Eighth—

To incorporate as organic architecture—so far as possible—furnishings, making them all one with the building and designing them in simple terms for machine work. Again straight lines and rectilinear forms.

Ninth—

Eliminate the decorator. He was all curves and all efflorescence, if not all "period." [1]

Architecturally speaking, all this meant a revolutionary concept of space. Peter Blake, managing editor of the *Architectural Forum,* writes that Wright's claim to greatness "rests squarely upon a single, staggering fact: Wright changed the nature of architectural space and then proceeded to change

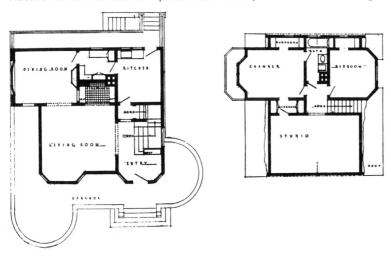

27
3. Wright house, plan, courtesy of Henry-Russell Hitchcock

the nature of structure and form to fit his new spatial concepts."[2] From the standpoint of the client, this approach meant that if he went to Wright, he got a house which *looked* different and *worked* differently from the conventional dwelling of the time. On the exterior it was immediately recognizable by its dramatic lines, by its broad overhanging eaves, and by the amount of glass which it utilized. On the interior it usually had no attic or basement, the heating, lighting, and plumbing were handled in new and unusual ways, and the sense of space was, of course, radically different. To understand what these innovations implied, it is only necessary to see one of these prairie houses standing among its more conventional neighbors. Obviously to become a Wright client required a special kind of enterprise.

It is only proper to say here that Wright did not achieve his revolution overnight. The early stages of his career were marked by a great deal of experimentation. During the eighteen nineties he designed in the Dutch Colonial, Tudor, and shingle styles, the last being a native interpretation of the Queen Anne. He owed something to Joseph Lyman Silsbee, in whose office he first worked when he came to Chicago, and much more to Louis Sullivan. Furthermore, in 1900, when he was, in Grant Manson's words, ready to "unveil the prairie house," he appeared to be only one of several capable young

28
4. Wright house, living room, courtesy of Chicago Architectural Photographing Co.

architects working along the same lines. The story of the informal club of progressive designers who met in Dwight Perkins' Steinway Hall offices is well known. Perkins, Robert Spencer, Myron and Jarvis Hunt, and George Dean were all members of this group. Each was in his own way determined to break away from the stylistic merry-go-round of nineteenth-century architecture and to find an expression that was both "personal" and "American." Later they were joined by such distinguished talents as George Maher, Walter Burley Griffin, William Gray Purcell, and George Grant Elmslie. Today we group these men together as "The Prairie School." Wright must thus be seen as the leader of a truly distinguished group of designers. To say this in no way detracts from his own achievement. It was he who had the courage and ability to push his ideas to the limit and thereby become a pathfinder for those who followed. In terms of reaction against established precedent he was by far the most radical, and he certainly had the greatest reputation among his contemporaries. It is therefore his clients who are most worthy of study. Our central question then becomes: What sort of person sponsors an architectural revolution? This is a query which has been suggested by most of the leading writers on Frank Lloyd Wright. Grant Manson, author of the authoritative *Frank Lloyd Wright: The First Golden Age,* remarks: "It is, in fact, amazing that Wright found

29
5. Wright house, dining room, courtesy of Chicago Architectural Photographing Co.

such a steady succession of clients willing to experiment and to try the uncharted."[3]

Some of Wright's success must, as Manson points out, be ascribed to his remarkable powers of persuasion. These were so great that they often excited the envy of his contemporaries; it is no exaggeration to say that he was one of the great salesmen of his age. Even a great salesman, however, will encounter difficulty when operating in a hostile environment. Any student of Wright's work will conclude that his environment from 1893, when he first entered independent practice, to the winter of 1915–1916, when he sailed for Japan to build the Imperial Hotel in Tokyo, was anything but hostile. Even the tremendous scandal of 1910, when he fled to Europe with Mamah Borthwick Cheney, deserting his wife and six children, was not enough to ruin him, nor was the terrible tragedy at Taliesin in 1913, when a crazed Negro servant set fire to the place, killing Mrs. Cheney and six other members of his household. Henry-Russell Hitchcock writes, "Wright was, in 1914 and 1915, far from being without work,"[4] and much the same comment could be made about the other members of the Prairie School, such as Purcell and Elmslie, Guenzel and Drummond, and George Maher. The real crisis for all these men came in 1916 or 1917, and with that phenomenon we will deal later.

30
6. Wright house, playroom, courtesy of Chicago Architectural Photographing Co.

Wright himself has given us a few clues about his clients. In a 1908 article for *Architectural Record* he wrote:

Even cultured men and women care so little for the spiritual integrity of their environment; except in rare cases they are not touched, they simply do not care for the matter so long as their dwellings are fashionable or as good as those of their neighbors and keep them dry and warm. A structure has no more meaning to them aesthetically than has the stable to the horse. And this came to me in the early years as a definite discouragement. There are exceptions, and I found them chiefly among American men of business with unspoiled instincts and untainted ideals. A man of this type usually has the faculty of judging for himself. He has rather liked the "idea" and much of the encouragement this work receives comes straight from him because the "common sense" of the thing appeals to him. While the "cultured" are still content with their small chateaux, Colonial wedding cakes, English affectations or French millinery, he prefers a poor thing but his own. He errs on the side of character, at least, and when the test of time has tried his country's development architecturally, he will have contributed his quota, small enough in the outcome though it be; he will be regarded as a true conservator.[5]

Wright suggests that his most sympathetic clients were "businessmen with unspoiled instincts and untainted ideals." What do these phrases convey? We submit that they imply (1) a certain freshness of vision and (2) lack of formal education. A man's instincts (or his native taste) had to be sound or he would not be able to see what Wright was trying to do. It is well known that Wright generally saw schools of all varieties as cor-

7. Wright house, leaded-glass detail, courtesy of Chicago Architectural Photographing Co.

rupting influences upon the human spirit, so it is not surprising that he speaks of "untainted" ideals. In this connection it is interesting to analyze the occupations and educations of these early clients.

Almost all can be classified as "businessmen." Within this broad category there is a fairly wide range of occupations; one finds bankers, brokers, real estate men, and various kinds of wholesale and retail merchants. The most striking aspect of the list, however, is the number who were manufacturers or directly involved in the industrial process. There were three physicians and three lawyers, though a scattering of the real estate and insurance people had law degrees. The relative lack of formal higher education is also important; in our compilation of forty clients, thirteen had achieved some kind of higher education, and this was almost always obtained at a state university. The unfortunate Edwin Cheney had a degree in electrical engineering from the University of Michigan, Meyer May finished two years at that institution, Walter Gale graduated from the University of Illinois in pharmacy and William Greene in engineering. Only Avery Coonley had a B.A. from an Ivy League school. The roster of Wright's clients is, in effect, a commentary on the fact that a college degree was not a necessity for business success in the United States prior to the First World War. Some of the most affluent of his clients, such as Jacob Walser and Edward Waller, had only a high school education. They were, in fact, men with "unspoiled instincts and untainted ideals."

At this point we may well ask: Were these clients perhaps self-educated men who derived unorthodox points of view from independent reading in the radical writers of their day? Were they, for example, followers of Henry George, Edward Bellamy, or Robert Ingersoll? Did they read the novels of Frank Norris and Theodore Dreiser or the poetry of Carl Sandburg and Vachel Lindsay? Here the answer is in the negative. In our study none of the sons and daughters made any reference to reading habits which were in any way unusual. Their parents read the daily newspapers, some of the mass circulation magazines of the period, an occasional novel or two, and that is about all. Their leisure time was, in fact, not ordinarily devoted to reading. Undoubtedly, most of them were acquainted with the giants of nineteenth-century American literature such as Emerson, Whitman, and Twain, but none were convinced followers of these men. It is unlikely that any of them were familiar with William Morris and Viollet-Le-Duc, writers from whom their architect drew intellectual sustenance. The clients preferred to spend their leisure hours at the country club, the music stand, or in the basement workshop. These latter avocations were of considerable significance.

A word is in order here concerning the economic status of these early clients. This is a matter which has been much misinterpreted in recent years, both by foreign critics and by Wright himself. At the time of Le Corbusier's death (1964) the Englishman Robert Furneaux Jordan wrote in the *London Observer,* "Of his colleagues, Lloyd Wright, the last romantic, built houses for Chicago millionaires." In 1952 Wright gave the following interview to a writer from the *New Yorker:*

Mr. Wright looked at us reproachfully, then went on, "my clients are from the upper section of the middle third of society — not from the mobocrats, at the bottom, or the Fascists, or Mr. Big, at the top. I guess I'm a big shot, and you know the big shot will never consult the big shot so Mr. Big goes to the little man in my field. He thinks it's smart to come in the back way. Well, it doesn't seem to be."

"Aren't the Guggenheims who run the Guggenheim Foundation big shots?" we asked.

"Solomon Guggenheim and Marshall Field are exceptions to the big shot rule. Both are aesthetic," said Mr. Wright.

"Isn't Edgar J. Kaufmann, the Pittsburg department store magnate for whom you built one of your famous private houses, a Mr. Big?" we asked, out of the depths of our architectural knowledge.

"Oh, no. He has only thirty or forty million dollars," said Mr. Wright, and he took us down to lunch.

It is probable that Jordan was simply misinformed or had never taken the trouble to look up the facts. Wright himself was doing something more complicated. He was projecting the clientele of his later years backward to encompass the patrons of his first two decades of practice. It was perhaps an understandable error, but it has obscured the true picture. That picture can only be obtained by studying the economic status of his patrons. They ranged all the way from families of genuinely modest means to moneyed aristocrats like the Coonleys, and there were a great many more of the former than of the latter. A surprising number of his most famous houses were built with small budgets. The Glasner house in Glencoe, done for $4500, is one good example, and the much admired Hardy house in Racine is another. In any event, what is significant about the group is that they did *not* seek to emulate the dwellings of the city's commercial leaders, whom we have elsewhere called the North Shore Establishment. This would have been the traditional method of achieving some of the status possessed by an existing aristocracy. On the contrary, they preferred to strike out on their own. This is especially noteworthy when it is considered that most were self-made men. Except for Avery Coonley and possibly the Beachy family, there are no examples of inherited wealth.

The lack of inherited wealth may have had a psychological effect which worked to Wright's benefit. As we have seen, most of his clients were self-made men. They were therefore highly mobile people within the structure of Chicago society. Now a number of studies have shown that mobile people are beset with certain psychological tensions. Since they have arrived only recently, they tend to be uncertain of the directions which they must take in order to ensure the maintenance of their new status. They are not precisely marginal to the culture in which they operate, but they certainly approach this condition. It may well be that this psychology of uncertainty was a strong factor in the decision of these men and women to employ Wright.

Besides the generalization that most of these clients were businessmen, we can say that the vast majority were Protestants and Republicans. There is, after all, nothing very surprising about this situation. Wright's clientele was essentially middle-class, and the entire American middle class of 1900–1914 tended to be white, Anglo-Saxon, Protestant, and in the Midwest, Republican. In any event, religion and politics were not, for most of Wright's clients, significant ways of defining social status and role. Among these men and women one finds all degrees of religious belief and disbelief, of activity and inactivity. Some of Wright's clients, particularly in Oak Park, obviously derived much satisfaction from working for their churches, while for others, church attendance was a matter of form. In a pluralistic society neither praise nor blame attaches to membership in a particular denomination, and it would therefore be a mistake to suggest that any of Wright's religiously liberal clients (Unitarians, Christian Scientists, and so on) built houses as gestures of social protest. If there is any connection between religious liberalism and architectural radicalism, it is tenuous. In fact, the clients themselves rarely attached any ideological significance to the design of their homes. For them the building of a new home was not a sign of adherence to an intellectual program. It was, as the daughter-in-law of one couple has written, simply a matter "of being able to enjoy the newest and the best of whatever enhanced good living." In this nonideological cast of mind the Wright clients unquestionably differed from the great patrons of the Gothic age and the Renaissance. In those periods there is a good deal of evidence to show that the new buildings did reflect complicated intellectual programs.

Much the same comment can be made about prairie architecture and the liberal political movements of the day. Within this milieu liberalism meant an acceptance of the progressive notions of Theodore Roosevelt and Woodrow Wilson. A small minority were enthusiastic about Roosevelt; almost none favored Wilson. In this connection it is interesting to note that very few of Wright's clients belonged to the class of small businessmen, frequently self-employed, whom Richard Hofstadter has identified as constituting the backbone of progressive strength in the Midwest.[6] One who did was O. B. Balch, a painting and decorating contractor in Oak Park, for whom Wright built a house in 1911. Balch employed about fifteen to twenty-five men and evidently worked on a certain number of Wright's houses. His daughter recalls that he was a tremendous admirer of Theodore Roosevelt at all times, including his Bull Moose phase. In fact, he frequently read aloud from Roosevelt's works to his children. Such loyalty, however, was the exception rather than the rule. Most of the early clientele were businessmen with offices in the Loop, and their politics were, figuratively speaking, formed on LaSalle Street, where liberalism has never been abundant. Probably the most progressive couple in the lot were the Avery Coonleys, whose liberalism had a background of inherited wealth and intellectual conviction.

On only one major issue of the day do these people seem to have generated much excitement: woman suffrage. A good many wives evidently felt strongly about this matter. Several sons and daughters now recall with some pride that their mothers marched as suffragettes down Michigan Avenue. Given the standards of the time, the entire group of clients impresses one as quite conventional. By far the most common family recreation was golf, and a large percentage of the clients belonged to one or more country clubs. A few belonged to the River Forest Tennis Club, and about the same number were members of the Art Institute. Edward Waller and Frank Thomas were prominent in this group. George Millard, for whom Wright built a small house in Highland Park in 1906, was the only member of a literary coterie, the Saints and Sinners. Head of the rare-book department at McClurg's, he was well known to book collectors and was a good friend of Eugene Field. None of the clients had any connections with the intellectuals at the University of Chicago, and it is likely that most of them would have been horrified by the ideas of Thorstein Veblen, who taught there from 1892–1906. Nonetheless, it should be noted here that Wright himself was well enough acquainted with the faculty of the university to become involved personally in the ill-fated Como Orchards scheme of 1908 in Montana, which was sponsored by a number of professors. It is also a matter of considerable interest that Wright built five houses near the university but none for professors.

Notwithstanding this apparent conventionality, the impression remains that we are dealing here with a group of vital, active men and women. On this point the testimony of Wright's second son is very clear. "All his clients," says John Lloyd Wright, "like his buildings, had style, snap, and were interesting." [7] He adds a good deal of colorful information on the marvelous Christmas parties at the Wallers' and his father's fondness for socializing:

Every Christmas for many years Dad's charming clients, Mr. and Mrs. E. C. Waller, gave a party for their friends, and all their children. It was held in the beautiful octagonal pavilion Dad designed for them. An all-glass arcade joined the pavilion to the house.

A fifteen foot Christmas tree, fully trimmed, cornucopias and all, sparkled in the center of the octagon. The sound of sleighbells signaled Santa's arrival with his bag of gifts which were passed out to each person by name. The grownups danced, the children played. Papa was always the life of the party. It seemed that the party was given for him and for the other children. It never started till he arrived and it ended when he left. Mrs. Waller was a gracious hostess. [8]

This passage conveys much of the style which Wright's clients possessed and which he himself had to an extraordinary degree. A man of enormous charm, he loved parties and was the life of any gathering he attended. A good many of his clients were similarly inclined; hence the large living rooms in the prairie houses. They were frankly intended as settings for parties.

In sum, we arrive at the conclusion that these people were conventional but not dull. In most respects their goals in life cannot be distinguished from those of the contemporary suburban bourgeoisie which did not build houses of advanced design. It would be difficult, for example, to differentiate sharply between the tastes and attitudes of the Heurtleys and the Hemingways, who lived within a few blocks of each other and were probably acquainted. Yet the Hemingways resided in a quite ordinary house, designed by Mrs. Hemingway in 1904, while the Heurtleys lived in one of Wright's masterpieces. What, then, caused Arthur Heurtley to commission Frank Lloyd Wright?

We would suggest that the answer to this complex query is to be sought along two lines: (1) Many of Wright's early clients had an aesthetic interest which, in the style of the period, was usually musical. Heurtley had a fine voice and was for several years president of a choral society. Winslow played the violin. Both the Thomases were fond of music, and Nathan Moore was chairman of his church's music committee. (2) A startling number of these clients were inventors. That is to say, they were directly involved in the industrial process as managers, and they contributed to it in a mechanical way. It is significant that most of these men were *not* affiliated with the large concerns which dominated Chicago industry—International Harvester, U.S. Steel, and so on. They tended to own or work for small and medium-sized companies, and as was the custom of the time, to be quite paternalistic in their outlooks. None belonged to the aristocracy of the city's business world. Among them one searches in vain for Ryersons, Armours, or McCormicks. Wright's only commission from this group, the great country house for Mr. and Mrs. Harold McCormick, fell through in circumstances which have never been satisfactorily explained. Of course, the generalization that the early clients were inventors will not hold in all cases. There were also plenty of brokers, insurance men, and realtors who had nothing whatever to do with invention. The important fact is that it holds for the key clients such as Robie and Winslow. These men obviously responded enthusiastically to Wright's own supremely inventive imagination. On the basis of the extant buildings, one would say that they were unusually willing to accept radical and daring solutions to their architectural programs.

Much has been written about the psychology of invention. A psychoanalyst says, "In every neurosis the early childhood sexual impulses, in all their original uncompromising power, strive for the primary aim, namely, union with the original love object. Inhibited, these strivings express themselves symbolically. Inventive ability may be considered one of these symbolic expressions." [9] The inventor is therefore somewhat like the artist in his ability to use and absorb conflict by a kind of controlled regression into the spontaneity of childhood. The French psychologist Joseph Marie Montmasson makes substantially the same point in his *Invention and the Unconscious* (London, 1931), but without an adequate definition or concep-

42

tion of the unconscious. Are we then to conclude that Wright's inventor clients were neurotics who compensated for their maladjustments by creative tinkering? In a few cases this may be true, but we still have no really good explanation for their astonishing receptivity to the new architecture. We believe that the most satisfying explanation is to be sought in the writings of a man who, curiously enough, was a close observer of the very people for whom Wright was designing his houses: the brilliant economist and sociologist Thorstein Veblen.

From 1892 to 1906 Veblen was a student and teacher in the economics department at the University of Chicago, and several writers have pointed out that much of his trenchant analysis of American economic life derives from his observation of the city's business world in those years. Most of his best work was done at Chicago, where he was surrounded by a group of faculty colleagues almost as brilliant as himself. It is an irony which would have pleased Veblen that certain passages from his *Theory of Business Enterprise* may help us to understand the attraction of Wright for his clientele. In the ninth chapter he writes:

Leaving aside the archaic vocations of war, politics, fashion, and religion, the employments in which men are engaged may be distinguished as pecuniary or business employments on the one hand, and industrial or mechanical employments on the other hand.[10]

43

This distinction between pecuniary and industrial employment is fundamental to Veblen's analysis of the place of the machine in modern society and is one of the most important which he ever made. Vocations, he argues, tend to create radically different outlooks on life:

The ultimate ground of validity for the thinking of the business classes is the natural rights ground of property — a conventional, anthropomorphic fact having an institutional validity, rather than a matter-of-fact validity such as can be formulated in terms of material cause and effect; while the classes engaged in the machine industry are habitually occupied with matters of causal sequence, which do not lend themselves to statement in anthropomorphic terms of natural rights and which afford no guidance in questions of institutional right and wrong, or of conventional reason and consequence. Arguments which proceed on material cause and effect cannot be met with arguments from conventional precedent or dialectically sufficient reason, and conversely.[11]

Stripped of its characteristic Veblenian jargon, the meaning of this passage is clear: the businessman, who is concerned with the making of money, will have a different outlook on life from the industrialist or technician who is concerned with the making of things.

No class, of course, is entirely exempt from pecuniary discipline. The engineer has to worry about profits and losses, and the businessman may be involved in the industrial process. Nonetheless, the distinction is generally sound. Even more

44

important is a corollary of Veblen's theory. "The thinking required by the pecuniary occupations," he writes, "proceeds on grounds of conventionality, whereas that involved in the industrial occupations runs, in the main, on grounds of mechanical sequence or causation, to the neglect of conventionality." [12] Hence, the business classes tend, on the whole, to be conservative. They, of course, are not alone in their conservatism; in comparison with them, the more archaic occupations of soldier, priest, and politician are positively reactionary. In contrast, the discipline of the machine, with its emphasis on materialistic reasoning, will tend to create a skepticism about established institutions.

If this line of thought is applied to Wright's early clientele, the choice of a "radical" architect becomes explicable in a certain number of important cases. Men like Robie, Winslow, and W. E. Martin were attracted to him because he seemed to think of architecture in terms that were familiar to them. In this connection the remark of Robie is especially significant. "When I talked in mechanical terms, he talked and thought in architectural terms. I thought, well, he was in my world." [13] On the basis of the available evidence, we suspect that certain others of Wright's clients might have used similar language if interviews were possible.

Reyner Banham supports this conjecture in an important

article entitled "Frank Lloyd Wright as Environmentalist" (*Architectural Design,* April 1967), in which he stresses the significance of heating, lighting, and ventilation as determinants in Wright's designs of this period. Chicago, says Banham, is, after all, located in the same latitude as Constantinople, and Wright took full advantage of the rather limited technology which was available to him to ensure his clients' physical comfort. Because the steam radiator was intrinsically an ugly object, he invariably boxed it in, but he located it for maximum environmental effect. Similar care was given to lighting and ventilation. It is no wonder, then, that many of the prairie houses still work well today.

The other feature of Wright's clientele which deserves comment is the extraordinary number of people who were musical. Wright himself was always conscious of the close relationship between his architecture and music. In his *Autobiography* he wrote that he was "always music hungry," and declared that "music and architecture blossom on the same stem: sublimated mathematics. Mathematics as presented by geometry. Instead of the musician's systematic staff and intervals, the architect has a modular system as the framework of design. My father, a preacher and music teacher, taught me to see—to listen—to a symphony as an edifice of sound." [14] In another passage he speaks of Bach as "the great architect who happened to choose music for his form." This is a description with which a good many musicologists would agree. Hans David and Arthur Mendel remark in their *Bach Reader,* "If Bach's desire to portray the emotions found its counterpart chiefly in the literature of his time, his concept of forms corresponds more closely to concepts realized in contemporary architecture." [15] More recently, Leonard Bernstein, writing of the music of Bach, cannot resist the architectural analogy. Commenting on the fifth Brandenburg Concerto he observes that "the rest of the movement will be a constant elaboration or reiteration of that main event just as the architecture of a bridge grows inevitably out of one initial arch." [16] Both Wright and these musicians seem to feel a common sense of form.

From the experimental psychologists come some intriguing confirmations of the close connection between musical and architectural perception. As long ago as 1919 Carl Seashore noted that musically talented students possessed high auditory imagery (the ability to re-create a tone image) and that this faculty was closely related to motor imagery and motor tendencies. These motor images are perceived in terms of feelings of effort and strain in the body. This kinesthetic response plays a large part in the enjoyment derived from active participation in music, architecture, and sport. Some modern physiologists have even set forth the view that there is an unlimited

47

cooperation of all parts of the nervous system in *every* activity. The German Von Cyon has located the temporal spatial and mathematical sensibilities in the ear. He holds that "the musical sense and the mathematical sense are functions of the same organ." [17] There is thus an actual physiological basis for the response of Wright's clients to the spatial and temporal qualities in architecture and music. The mathematical correlation might explain the presence of inventors in their works. The presence of so many musical organizations in Oak Park is therefore an item of more than casual interest.

In this connection it is well to note that Wright's interest in Bach and Beethoven was in a sense a continuation of Sullivan's fascination with Wagner and that musical life in late-nineteenth-century America exhibited almost the same polarity as architecture, with the neo-classicists centered in Boston and the Wagnerites in Chicago. The references to Wagner in the *Autobiography of an Idea* demonstrate that Sullivan came close to G. B. Shaw's definition of the "Perfect Wagnerite," whose discipleship rested on the simple premise that "if the sound of the music has any power to move you, you will expect nothing more." [18] Sullivan's response to Wagner was made in terms of the sound experience itself, and there are many analogies between the expressive effects of Wagner's music and his own architecture. Furthermore, he was exposed to a tremendous amount of Wagner in Chicago; the programs of Hans Balatka and Theodore Thomas reflect an enormous enthusiasm for Wagner in the city. In Boston, on the other hand, the field was held by traditionalists. In the late eighteen sixties, John Knowles Paine, teaching a course at Harvard entitled "The History of Music to the Death of Schubert," remarked that the future of the art lay in an adherence to the forms of Bach, Mozart, Handel, and Beethoven. In 1895 Daniel Gregory Mason, leader of the Boston school of composers, wrote in his journal, "Thank God Wagner is dead and Brahms alive. And here's to the great classical revival of the 20th century in America." [19] The parallels are too striking to be ignored.

Needless to say, the foregoing is not a complete explanation of Wright's clientele. A good many people were attracted to him by sheer propinquity in Oak Park and by his enormous personal charm. It is not too much to say that in certain circles his style was for a little while actually fashionable. We can conclude, however, that it made a special appeal to the independent, technologically minded businessmen with a taste for music somewhere in the family. In the Chicago of 1893–1913 there were a good many such people. The twentieth century has seen technology become more and more the concern of a specialized class. As industrial concentrations have grown in size, their research and development sections have also grown.

Today's corporate manager is much less likely to be intimately involved in the industrial process than he was early in the century. He will probably be expert in marketing, in finance, or in some other business speciality. Hence he will lack the amazing open-mindedness which characterized so many of Wright's clients. Like J. P. Marquand's Willis Wayde, the prototype of the contemporary corporate tycoon, he will live in a traditional mansion and collect antique furniture. The new modern client is an entirely different sort of person.

How do Wright's clients of 1893–1913 compare in personality and life-style with a typical group of modern clients? According to Irving Rosow, who studied twenty-one such clients intensively in 1948, the ideal client couple will be college graduates, and the husband will be a professional man (lawyer or doctor) or teacher in the classic sciences, arts, or social sciences. The wife will also have an occupational identification with a professional or creative field; she will either be working or intend to work when conditions at home permit. They will be affiliated with four or five organizations, of which at least one or two will express their own individual interests; often they will be involved with adult education programs or organizations for the promotion of culture. Politically, the couple will be liberal and could probably be classified as New Dealers. Leisure time will be spent mainly in personal interest activities on an individual basis and in social intercourse with friends and family. Personal interest functions are encouraged and not construed as centrifugal forces tearing apart the family's common ground and group unity. The couple's main entertainment interests lie in the theater and concert hall, and they are apt to be season ticket holders. Aside from theaters and concerts, they are subjected to an almost constant diet of music and books. One or the other paints, sculpts, plays an instrument, writes, or engages in purposive study. They also spend a good deal of time on sports, travel, and puttering about house and garden. They have substantial libraries and record collections, eschew the Hearst magazines and tabloids, and in addition to professional journals, subscribe to such upper-middlebrow periodicals as *Harper's,* the *Atlantic Monthly,* and the *Saturday Review.* They entertain frequently and informally, and the family is of the equalitarian, democratic type with a high degree of harmony. In short, Rosow finds that "the modern client is a strongly individuated deviant whose security and satisfaction derive largely from individual definitions. The house is a means to a personally desired life activity pattern." [20] It is definitely *not* an instrument for the achievement of social status.

In certain respects the Wright clients of 1893–1913 obviously prefigure this ideal modern type. For example, the fond-

51

ness for music is easily recognizable in the Winslows, Moores, and Thomases, and certainly a good many of the early clients spent their leisure time in sporting activities, chiefly golf. On the other hand, very few were liberals politically, and only a handful of the women had a professional or creative orientation. A small minority of the men were professional people. The vast majority were businessmen, frankly engaged in making money. The organizations to which they belonged were chiefly country clubs, athletic clubs in downtown Chicago, and the like, not associations for the furtherance of some creative recreational specialty. Only a few were members of the Art Institute, and except for some who became interested in Japanese prints through Wright himself, none were art collectors. In certain respects this lack of interest was probably fortunate. James Fitch has brilliantly demonstrated the basis of Wright's well-founded skepticism about modern painting and sculpture.[21] It would have been ludicrous for him to design houses as containers for Bouguereaus and Rosa Bonheurs.

Wright's clients of 1893–1915 were, then, a group of middle-class businessmen with a small sprinkling of professional people. Outwardly conventional, they nonetheless tended to possess a streak of artistic or technological interest which predisposed them to accept new and radical solutions to the architectural problem of the dwelling house. The programs for their residences, however, tended to be conventional, as the men and women themselves were conventional. The average family was small, consisting of husband, wife, and two or three children; among the more affluent, quarters for a servant would be included in the planning. A program including three or four bedrooms, living room, dining room, kitchen, and bath was therefore usual. If a family had special interests, a music room or library would be added. Because Wright's clients tended to be sociable people (the Wallers and Winslows are good examples), the allotment of space for living rooms was often substantial. All of this amounted to the kind of program which is still common today, and may explain the fact that many of the prairie houses are still in use as dwellings, giving excellent satisfaction to new owners. At Wright's death in 1959 the Chicago papers were filled with photographs of his various structures in the area. One of them, the Emil Bach house at 7415 N. Sheridan Road, was occupied by Dr. Manuel Weiss. In an interview with the *Chicago Sun-Times* Dr. Weiss said, "Even though Mr. Wright designed the house in 1915, it has all the features of contemporary houses. Our eight years here have been delightful." Many people in Oak Park and River Forest would make much the same comment.

The prairie houses therefore stand in stark contradistinction to a great body of modern architecture in Europe. While

53

few systematic studies of the early patrons of the Modern Movement on the Continent have ever been done, it is clear that most of them had very little in common with the suburban clients of Wright. For example, most of the men who supported Henry Van de Velde during his Brussels, Berlin, and Weimar years (1896–1914) were, to a startling extent, continuators of the grand European tradition of aristocratic patronage. One thinks immediately of Harry, Count Kessler. Of German origin, but educated in Paris and London, Kessler had the type of manners cultivated at Ascot, and was completely at home in the most brilliant salons of the great European capitals. An early admirer of Van de Velde and visitor to his home at Bloemenwerf, he played an important role in securing the appointment of the young Belgian artist to the court of the grand duke of Saxe-Weimar. A serious student of contemporary art, Kessler had an important collection of post-Impressionist pictures, and did much to bring the achievement of French artists to the attention of the German public. Eberhard Von Bodenhausen was a similarly international personality. Born of an American mother and a German father whose lineage went back to the Teutonic knights, he was one of the founders of *Pan,* a journal devoted to the cause of Jugendstil, and like Kessler, took a deep interest in contemporary art. Von Bod-

54

enhausen was also an ardent supporter of Van de Velde and is spoken of with affection in the artists' autobiography. Karl Ernst Osthaus, for whom Van De Velde did the interior of the Folkwang Museum at Hagen and an imposing villa outside the town in 1908, belonged to the German *"grosse Bürgertum,"* a class only slightly less exalted than the hereditary aristocracy. In outlook and personality these men could hardly differ more radically from Wright's clients of 1893–1913.

In the post-World War I era the patrons of Le Corbusier offer another interesting comparison. This group was not titled but seems to have been composed mostly of eccentrics, art collectors, and various other kinds of avant-gardists. From Le Corbusier they commissioned a series of dwellings which were profoundly influential on the Modern Movement. The programs, of course, differed sharply from those presented by Wright's customers. Can one imagine the aesthetic Leo Stein, for whom the superb villa at Garches was done in 1927, living in Oak Park or River Forest? Hardly. The art dealer La Roche who, with Le Corbusier's cousin Albert Jeanneret, commissioned an important double house in 1923, would have been equally out of place. The central feature of the La Roche house is a two-story living room filled with first-class School of Paris pictures; it contains a handsome staircase by which the owner could make his entrance to some extremely Bohemian parties. The sculptor Jacques Lipchitz was another client from this period. His house was mostly studio.

This is not to denigrate the marvelous architectural quality of these buildings in any way. It is merely an attempt to set them (and those of Wright) in their proper context. The truth of the matter is that Le Corbusier's clients were, to a very large extent, eccentrics and enthusiasts for the more advanced varieties of modern art. Hence the programs with which they presented him were, to say the least, unusual. In this light some of the features of these houses which are otherwise quite puzzling become understandable; the roof gardens for sunbathing in a climate where this is possible only a few days per year are a good example. It is simply impossible to imagine any of Wright's early clients including a sundeck as part of their program.

It is also possible to comprehend, in part at least, Le Corbusier's peculiar failure to be influential in the United States. He was designing houses for a class of people which, with the exception of a few tiny enclaves here and there, simply does not exist in this country. Wright, on the other hand, was designing houses for members of the vast American middle class. This was a class to which he himself belonged for a good many

56

years and whose needs, both physical and psychological, he understood profoundly. Hence his houses of 1893–1913 are full of useful precedents which have all too often been ignored by contemporary designers, hypnotized by one or another of the dogmas which beset modern architecture. The most obvious of these is his use of glass. No one understood better than Wright that glass was a wonderful material, but no one was more conscious that in the American climate it generally needed to be protected by a deep overhang. Otherwise the sun would make life in the house unbearable. How many contemporary architects have taken into account this simple but important fact?

We hasten to add that the foregoing is not intended to reduce architectural criticism to a consideration of how well the designer has solved his client's functional program. It is merely to suggest that all sound criticism must begin with this consideration and progress from it to questions of architectonic form, symbolic expression, and the like. Architecture, after all, begins with a request from an individual client to a specific architect for a particular kind of building. This generalization will hold true even for the building programs of large corporations, which are customarily turned over to giant firms such as Skidmore, Owings, and Merrill. Architectural criticism

should, therefore, begin as Reyner Banham has recently remarked, with a study of how well the architect has handled the
"ascertainable brief." [22]

Seen in this light, Wright's prairie houses are, for the most
part, an overwhelming success. Not only did Wright solve his
clients' functional programs, he produced great architecture
in the process. There is, after all, an enormous difference between the provision of a large living room for the entertainment of family and friends and the design of such magnificent
spaces as Wright created for the Coonleys, the Martins, the
Robies, and many other clients. One proof of his success is
the continuing friendship of many of these people with their
architect. Most of them appear to have been well satisfied
with the job which he did for them. Some, like Charles Roberts,
actually became apostles of the new architecture. A satisfied
client can give no stronger endorsement.

We should also note the thoroughly businesslike transactions between Wright and his prairie clients. Most of these
houses seem to have been built within the construction esti-
mate. Frederick C. Robie refers to the building of his house
as "one of the cleanest business deals I ever had," and Herbert Angster and William Greene, who built Wright houses in
1911 and 1912, make substantially the same remark. Angster
says, "I was more impressed with the execution than the de-

58

sign of the house—and I loved the design. Every board, every brick was examined. He was not like most architects: he was always on the job, concerned with every detail." [23] The weight of the evidence, then, is that at this time of his life Wright was as careful with his clients' pocketbooks as he was with his own design. Of course, like most architects, he was happy when he had a lot of money to spend, as in the Coonley and D. D. Martin houses, but he was perfectly capable of watching the pennies on a small job like the O. B. Balch house in Oak Park of 1911. Here he knew very well that the client could not afford any extravagances.

One of the many paradoxes in Wright's career is that these scrupulous business practices toward his clients were accompanied by spendthrift personal habits and a notable lack of regard for his staff and family. John Lloyd Wright has recounted a typical episode involving a sheriff attempting to collect a debt of $1500 from his father in 1913. While the son stalled the sheriff in the drafting room, the father managed to sell a rare set of wood-block color prints to a collector for $10,000. After settling the debt, Wright senior proceeded to Marshall Field's, where he ordered a dozen armchairs at $125.00 each and a dozen Chinese rugs, and then to Lyon and Healy's, where he purchased three grand pianos. They finished the day with a gourmet dinner at the Pompeiian Room of the

Congress Hotel. "The inner man satisfied," says Wright junior, "Dad leaned back in his chair—the picture of serene contentment. It had been a perfect day, he had succeeded in plunging himself into debt again and everything was normal once more." [24] Grant Manson is likewise very clear that paychecks at the Oak Park studio were, by 1909, extremely irregular, and a recent article on William Drummond states, rather delicately, that he worked for Wright as long as he could afford to. Notwithstanding these financial irregularities, the available testimony is that Wright's business dealings with his early clients were straightforward and correct.

Did Wright's clients themselves contribute anything to the architectural revolution? This is a question of great interest to the historian. The answer must be sought along two lines. The more technologically minded among them probably did make certain suggestions which affected the design. Wright's attitude toward his work fascinated these men, and some of them became directly involved in it. W. E. Martin, for example, became so intrigued that he used to drive Wright around to inspect his various jobs; on one occasion Wright kept him waiting two hours outside the Coonley residence. The Robie interview makes clear that the steel beams which make possible the extended cantilevers of the roof plane were suggested by the client, not the architect. How much of this sort of thing there was we shall never know, since most of the early clients have died. Wright, of course, must receive the credit for adopting what were probably very sensible notions.

More important and much more subtle was the impact on Wright of the kind of program which he received from these clients. The strength and clarity of these programs are again most evident in the Robie interview, but are echoed in a large number of other case histories. For the most part these clients were strong-minded, straight-thinking individuals who knew what they wanted. Few possessed inherited wealth; most had made their own modest fortunes. They may be regarded as prototypes of David Riesman's inner-directed individuals, who abounded to such an extraordinary degree during the nineteenth century. While they were willing to give due regard to Wright's professional competence as an architect, they did not see him as a genius whose every whim had divine inspiration and had to be obeyed. William Greene didn't hesitate to argue with Wright about various aspects of his house, but he found that Wright was usually correct. Greene had his way about the roof, which Wright had wanted to keep flat. Grant Manson has remarked that Wright owed much to the skillful craftsmen who carried out his striking ideas. Similarly we would contend that he also owed something to a group of clients who gave him programs that were both clear and challenging.

We have, then, a picture of the typical Wright client of 1893–1915 as a businessman who owns at least a part of his own middle-sized manufacturing concern. He will probably not be a college graduate, and if he does have higher education, it will have been obtained at a state university. Though most of his time is devoted to the management of his company, he is likely to be well acquainted with the technological side of the business. He may be an inventor himself; in any event, his interest in technology is a factor in opening up his mind to architectural innovation. If he is not familiar with the industrial process, an interest in technology is apt to be displayed in some hobby such as photography. Interest in arts other than architecture is usually shown in a fondness for music. He, or someone in his immediate family, will sing or play an instrument. Probably he has no knowledge of sculpture or painting, and he is not likely to be a member of the circle which actively supports the Institute. His standard forms of recreation are golf and tennis.

In religion he will almost certainly be Protestant, and he may be either lukewarm or devout. He will support his church financially and will be a member in good standing, though he may not often attend. In politics he is, of course, Republican and is likely to be a follower of Theodore Roosevelt. While admiring Roosevelt, however, he will probably not follow him into the Bull Moose movement of 1912. Though not himself devoted to liberal causes, he will display an easy tolerance if his wife becomes a suffragette. He will not be particularly tolerant of eccentric social behavior. He will be shocked by Wright's affair with Mrs. Cheney, though he may retain the architect's friendship in later years. In his own family he is a commanding figure but not the heavy father of Victorian tradition. It would be inaccurate to say that family decisions are reached democratically. He usually takes the lead and is apt to be the instigator of the house-building project. This makes him sound quite conventional, and it is intended to do so. The final paradox of the Wrightian revolution is this: like the American upheaval of 1776–1783, it was sponsored by people who were basically conservative.

2 Footnotes

[1] Frank Lloyd Wright, "Prairie Architecture" in *Frank Lloyd Wright: Writings and Buildings,* ed. Edgar Kaufman and Ben Raeburn, (New York, 1960), pp. 45–47.
[2] Peter Blake, "Frank Lloyd Wright: Master of Architectural Space," *Architectural Forum,* (CIX, September 1958), p. 121.
[3] Grant Manson, *Frank Lloyd Wright to 1910: The First Golden Age* (New York, 1958), p. 68.

[4] Henry-Russell Hitchcock, *In the Nature of Materials* (London, 1941), p. 67.

[5] Frank Lloyd Wright, "In the Cause of Architecture," *Architectural Record* (XXIII, 1908), p. 158.

[6] Richard Hofstadter, *The Age of Reform* (New York, 1955; Vintage ed. 1960), pp. 131–173.

[7] John Lloyd Wright, *My Father Who Is on Earth* (New York, 1946), p. 42.

[8] *Ibid.,* pp. 40–41.

[9] Sandor Lorand, "A Note on the Psychology of the Inventor," *Psychoanalytic Quarterly* (III, 1934), p. 30.

[10] Thorstein Veblen, *The Theory of Business Enterprise,* as quoted in Max Lerner, *The Portable Veblen* (New York, 1958), p. 341.

[11] *Ibid.,* p. 344.

[12] *Ibid.*

[13] "Mr. Robie Knew What he Wanted," *Architectural Forum* (CIX, 1958), p. 127.

[14] Frank Lloyd Wright, *An Autobiography* (London, 1946), p. 201.

[15] Hans David and Arthur Mendel, *The Bach Reader* (New York, 1945), p. 42.

[16] Leonard Bernstein, *The Joy of Music* (New York, 1959), p. 231.

[17] E. V. Cyon, *"Das Ohrlabyrinth als Organ der mathematischen Sinne der Raum und Zeit"* (Berlin, 1908), quoted in *Reflections on Art,* ed. Suzanne Langer (New York, 1961), p. 268.

[18] Bernard Shaw, *The Perfect Wagnerite* (London, 1913), pp. 4–5.

[19] Gilbert Chase, *America's Music* (New York, 1955), p. 365.

[20] Irving Rosow, *Modern Architecture and Social Change,* M.A. thesis (1948), Wayne State University, pp. 160–168.

[21] James Fitch, *Architecture and the Aesthetics of Plenty* (New York, 1961), pp. 104–123.

[22] Reyner Banham, *Convenient Benches and Handy Hooks — Functional Considerations in the Criticism of the Art of Architecture,* Unpublished address delivered at the joint AIA–ACSA Conference at Cranbrook School, June 12, 1964.

[23] Herbert Angster in a telephone interview, March 24, 1964.

[24] John Lloyd Wright, *My Father,* p. 78.

3 Profiles of Wright Clients

In order to convey the personalities of Wright's clients in the period 1893–1913, we have included here a series of thirteen profiles of clients who came to the Oak Park Studio during these years. They are chosen to show the range of his practice, the economic bracket for which he worked, and the sort of person who sought out his services. The profiles focus on such vital matters as religion, politics, occupation, family life, and leisure-time activity. Where these are available, we have given details on the actual business transactions between Wright and these clients in an effort to elucidate their relationships.

Mr. and Mrs. William Herman Winslow (River Forest, Illinois, 1893)

Ills. pp. 67–71

William H. Winslow was Frank Lloyd Wright's first important client after his departure from the office of Adler and Sullivan, and he is therefore a figure of great interest. In his occupation, outlook of life, and leisure-time activities he set the pattern for many who were to come to the Oak Park studio.

Born of Danish immigrant parents in Brooklyn, New York, in 1857, Winslow numbered several clergymen and scholars among his ancestors. His family moved about a good bit, and he was educated in the public schools of Brooklyn and Chicago. While he never went to college, he did study law in New York; it is probable that he simply read law in the office of an

67
1. W. H. Winslow,
courtesy of Miss
Mina Winslow

established attorney. This was a common approach to the profession in those days. In any event, the law made no appeal to him, and in 1881 he went to work for the Hecla Iron Works of New York as office man. He remained with this firm for four years, becoming a partner in 1883 at the age of twenty-six. This rapid rise in the business world is, of course, typical of many careers in post-Civil War America. In 1885 a better opportunity opened up in Chicago, and he joined E. T. Harris in that city to form the firm of Harris and Winslow, manufacturers of ornamental iron and bronze. A few years later Harris retired, and Winslow associated with his brother Francis in a new concern, Winslow Brothers. Their business prospered and ultimately had offices in New York City (160 Fifth Avenue), Baltimore, Pittsburgh, New Orleans, Minneapolis, Kansas City, Los Angeles, and San Francisco. It is important to note that Winslow's wealth and social position were achieved rather than inherited. His house itself, of course, is the best evidence for the solid affluence of its owner, which was expressed with dignity rather than conspicuous display.

In many respects William H. Winslow (his family and friends always called him Herman) seems to have been a typical businessman of his time. His politics were Republican, and he never appears to have had any sympathy for the progressive movement, which transformed American political life during

68
2. Winslow house, front elevation, courtesy of Henry-Russell Hitchcock

the early years of the century. Like a good many of Wright's clients, he was a liberal in religious matters, being a member of the Society for Ethical Culture. Rather shy in his social relations, he was one of those people who are almost equally happy in the company of others and alone. He limited his club memberships to the Union League and Cliff Dwellers in Chicago. In his youth he apparently had a taste for military life, since he was a member of the 13th Regiment of the New York National Guard. His family life was harmonious. In 1891 he married Edith Henry of St. Louis, a lively and charming woman who organized the social life which he himself was probably too diffident to provide. Their marriage was blessed with two boys and a girl, who grew up happily in the famous house which Wright built for the family in 1893.

It was business which brought Wright and Winslow together, and it is appropriate to pay some attention to the nature of the firm and Winslow's role in it. Winslow Brothers made bronze- and iron-work for architects all over the country and took a deep pride in the high quality of its products. The output consisted of such objects as elevator grills, stair railings, memorial tablets, and the like. Among its noteworthy achievements were the famous rounded corner entryway on the Carson, Pirie, Scott Store by Louis Sullivan and the elevator grills in the Rookery by Frank Lloyd Wright. According to Wright's *Auto-*

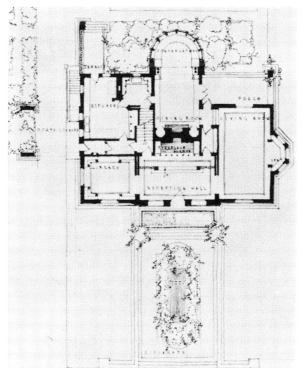

69
3. Winslow house, ground-floor plan, courtesy of Henry-Russell Hitchcock

biography, Winslow made his acquaintance during the course of an earlier job for Adler and Sullivan. That he went to Wright when the latter was only twenty-six and just starting out in independent practice is sufficient comment on the acuteness of his perceptions.

Much more than the ordinary industrial manager of our day, Winslow entered into the technological side of his business. Both he and his brother Francis made contributions to the bronze- and iron-casting process, and they invented the Winslow window, a pioneering variety of movable sash. They also worked on a flash boiler for the steam automobile. This was an immediate concern, since they both drove steam cars. Winslow was, in fact, an inventor and a man who all his life was fascinated by things mechanical. His daughter recalls her childhood as being filled with mechanical devices. These included elaborate swings and gymnastic apparatus and an auto turntable in the garage, which she and her brothers used as a merry-go-round, somewhat to their parents' displeasure.

Winslow's other hobbies reveal a still deeper interest in craftsmanship and invention. A good cabinetmaker, he loved to work in wood and must certainly have responded to Wright's emphasis on the nature of materials. He was sufficiently interested in the craft of printing to require space for his own press as part of his architectural program. Together with his dark-

70
4. Winslow children and friends

room (for he was also a photographer), it was lodged in the basement of the house. The best known product of this press was a handsome publication of W. C. Gannett's *The House Beautiful.* The original is a collector's item, and it has recently been reissued in a facsimile edition. Frank Lloyd Wright did the page decorations and Winslow the typography and binding.

In addition to these interests, Winslow was an excellent musician who played the violin well to the end of his life. His daughter, Mrs. John Briggs, was for many years head of the piano department at Hamline University in St. Paul, and she attributes her ability as a fast reader and good accompanist entirely to her father's desire to use her as his accompanist at an early age. There can be no question about Winslow's seriousness as a musician. He practiced scales and exercises for half an hour in the morning before he went to work, and then played for an hour or so in the evening. It is significant that the few conflicts which the Winslow family displayed arose apropos of music. Mrs. Briggs recalls the only harsh words which her father addressed to her as occurring when she failed to accompany him properly in a piece for piano and violin. He addressed her sharply, she burst into tears, he put his arms around her, and all was forgiven. Winslow was, she says, too reserved to enjoy his children greatly when they were young. He had to wait for them to grow up. Since Brother Francis

71
5. W. H. Winslow practicing violin

played the cello and his wife the piano, there were a good many family concerts in the large living room which lies on axis with the main entrance of the house. In fact, the window-seats which line the projecting bay make it into a kind of tiny theater. Evidently a streak of artistic talent runs throughout the Winslow family. Francis was a gifted draftsman who delighted in caricature, and his daughter, Miss Mina Winslow, is a fine amateur painter.

The Winslow family was both close-knit and extremely sociable. Mrs. Winslow enjoyed entertaining, and was noted for her Fourth of July parties. Frank Lloyd Wright usually came over from Oak Park for these celebrations, an indication that he stayed on good terms with the family. Together with their neighbors the Edward Wallers, for whom Wright built an apartment house in 1895, they combined to give large Christmas parties. The property was large enough to accommodate a toboggan slide in the backyard, and there were a good many neighborhood tobogganing parties for the children in the winter. Miss Mina Winslow still recalls the wonderful effect of the grate fire in the entryway on a cold winter day. She recalls her uncle's outstanding characteristic as being his optimism. No matter how badly things may have looked at the moment (and the Winslow firm had to weather two serious business depressions, 1893 and 1907), he was certain that everything would turn out well in the end. It is pleasant to note that the Winslow house served the family well for more than twenty years, by which time the children had grown up and moved away from home. It is still beautifully maintained today by the present owners, Mr. and Mrs. William Walker.

We thus have a picture of a capable businessman with a strong feeling for craftsmanship and invention and a definitely artistic turn of mind. It is a portrait surprisingly like that of Sinclair Lewis' Sam Dodsworth, who was fond of Beethoven and had a Mary Cassatt portrait in his library. Like Winslow, Dodsworth was immersed in the technical details of his business and much concerned with the quality of his product, the Revelation automobile. He took real pride in keeping the price down to the very lowest level at which his kind of car could be built,[1] and he accepted the necessity of selling out to the giant Unit Automotive Company with obvious distaste. In addition, Dodsworth thought well of Dreiser and Cabell, and made a serious effort to understand architecture during his various European wanderings. One cannot help thinking that he and Winslow would have understood each other very well.

In context of this analysis, Winslow's most important quality was, of course, his extraordinary willingness to accept Wright's revolutionary design. Here he went far beyond Dodsworth, who lived in a thoroughly conventional mansion. Their mutual fondness for craftsmanship undoubtedly bound him to Wright, and his interest in invention certainly made him willing to accept a good many of the young man's daring proposals. Beyond these obvious factors, however, one senses in William Winslow a certain boldness which is unusual in clients during any age. He was a sensitive man, and Wright relates that he endured a mild variety of persecution from his conservative friends after his house was finished. "For a few months," says Grant Manson, "he avoided the popular morning and evening expresses on the railway to escape the banter of the scores of commuters who knew him well enough to speak their minds." [2] To commission and carry through this kind of house in the eighteen nineties required both perception and courage.

Mr. and Mrs. Nathan Grier Moore (Oak Park, Illinois, 1895)
The comments on Nathan G. Moore in Wright's *Autobiography* are distinctly unflattering and belie the true facts of their relationship. Wright relates that Moore came to him at a time when his three young children lacked proper shoes and thus was able to secure the English half-timber house which he wanted. "At any rate," he says, "it was the one time in the course of a long career that I gave in to the fact that I had a family and they had a right to live—and their living was up to me." [3] This is true as far as it goes, but Wright neglects to men-

tion that he and Moore were true kindred spirits, that Moore used to relax by playing the piano in Wright's studio, and that not even the Cheney scandal destroyed their friendship.

Born in Pennsylvania in 1853, Moore was a graduate of Lafayette College who moved west to practice law, at first in Peoria and later with considerable success in Chicago. He specialized in real estate work and also numbered the Chicago and North Western Railroad among his clients. It is interesting to note that his partner, John P. Wilson, Jr., later built a distinguished townhouse by Howard Van Doren Shaw. The two lawyers were, however, essentially different types of personality, and the houses which they built for themselves were correspondingly at variance. The vital, if rather confused, Moore house has little in common with the elegant English creation of Shaw. The son of a clergyman, Moore was a devout Presbyterian, an elder, and chairman of the music and building committees of his church. Like the vast majority of Wright's clients, he was a conventional Republican but did not interest himself in national affairs except to vote regularly. He was, however, active in local politics and for some years was chairman of the Oak Park School Board. A sociable couple, the Moores entertained a good deal, and at their parties there was usually a lot of singing around the piano. Music, in fact, was Moore's great avocation. Before entering on a legal career he had been an organ salesman, and his practice of auditioning choir candidates for the Presbyterian church in his downtown law office gave rise to much good-natured joking among his associates. He also played a good game of golf and was a longtime member of the Oak Park Country Club. Finally, he was a photography enthusiast and had his own darkroom. Among Wright's clients outside the field of manufacturing, one will often find the assertion of a scientific or technological interest as a hobby. Moore was sufficiently interested in photography to haul the heavy cameras of those days halfway up Pikes Peak to obtain good pictures.

Moore's story is included here to illustrate some of the problems involved in making an accurate assessment of Wright's relationships with his clients. If we relied on the *Autobiography* alone, it would be impossible to tell that the architect remained on cordial terms with Moore. The most telling evidence on this point is that his son-in-law, Edward R. Hills, built a Wright house in Oak Park in 1901. This case is also a good illustration of the really quite conventional character of the majority of Wright's clients. We err if we see them as being in any way out of sympathy with the period in which they lived. Most of them were happy with the social, cultural, and political milieu in which they found themselves. In Wright's prairie architecture there is no desire whatever to *"épater la bour-*

geoisie." On the contrary, it was perfectly adapted to the needs and tastes of a particular segment of the bourgeoisie.

Mr. and Mrs. Charles E. Roberts (Oak Park, Illinois, 1896)

While Frank Lloyd Wright never did any great amount of building for Charles E. Roberts, his importance to the architect was much greater than a modest volume of business would indicate. In 1896 Wright began the remodeling of the interior of the Roberts residence, which extended over a period of years. He also built a stable for this client, which is today converted into a residence. The significance of Roberts lies in the fact that he was the most active member of the building committee of the Oak Park Universalist Church. In his *Autobiography* Wright remarks that "he was the strong man in this instance or Unity Temple would never have been built." [4] Evidently the Roberts family were quite devout; each night before he went to bed Mr. Roberts would sit down at the piano and play and sing a hymn. Second, his daughter, Isabel Roberts, became a sort of general factotum at Wright's Oak Park studio. She kept the books and even occasionally tried her hand at design. For her, Wright built the lovely house in River Forest (1908) which has been so much admired and so widely published. Third, Mrs. B. Harley Bradley of Kankakee was the sister of Mrs. Roberts, and for her Wright built one of the first true prairie houses (1900). Warren Hickox of the same city was her brother, and Roberts was responsible for obtaining both the Bradley and Hickox commissions. He was thus a true proselytizer for Wright—convinced of his greatness and eager to secure jobs for him. It should also be noted that the Robertses were close friends of the Furbecks, for whom Wright built two houses in Oak Park.

In his business life, Roberts perfectly exemplifies the striking vein of invention which occurs in many of Wright's most important clients. He was the founder and president of the American Steel Screw Company, which was and is one of the largest of its kind in the United States. Himself an inventor, he designed many of the machines of the screw industry, some of which are still in use. When he died at age ninety-three, plans on which he was then engaged were found in his basement workshop, and these plans were subsequently developed into a useful and profitable piece of machinery. As one might suspect, he spent most of his time in that workshop and had relatively little taste for entertaining. His wife, on the other hand, enjoyed society. Despite this conflict between the two, the marriage was harmonious. Mr. and Mrs. Roberts adjusted nicely to their divergent interests.

How did the Robertses come to engage Frank Lloyd Wright to remodel their house? Very simply, they were friends and neighbors. Living a few blocks from The Studio, Roberts came to admire Wright's work at an early date, and soon presented him with the opportunity to remodel his house. Subsequently the families became good friends, and Roberts actually sent his son Chapin to the Hillside Home School, run by Wright's aunts in Spring Green, Wisconsin. Even the Cheney scandal did not interrupt the relationship. Although no details of the transactions survive, it appears that Roberts helped Wright financially at various times. On his part, Wright remembered his old friend by naming a room at Taliesin West after him. In sum, Roberts is typical of the loyal clients in Oak Park who built up for Wright a true structure of patronage.

Mr. and Mrs. W. E. Martin (Oak Park, Illinois, 1903)

One day in 1903 W. E. Martin of Oak Park and his brother Darwin of Buffalo, New York, were out driving. They passed The Studio, and intrigued by its appearance stopped to call on the owner. That same afternoon Wright received a commission for a house from W. E. and shortly thereafter was summoned to Buffalo to undertake an important series of commissions for Darwin D. Martin and his associates in the Larkin Company, a pioneer in the mail-order business. These commissions included houses for Martin himself (1904), for W. R. Heath (1905), and Walter V. Davidson (1908), and most important of all, the famous Larkin Building (1904), which served as the company's administrative headquarters. This structure was unquestionably one of the most significant buildings in the entire history of the Modern Movement and was especially influential in Europe. It is interesting to note that Mrs. Heath was the sister of Elbert Hubbard, a personality whom Wright resembled in many ways. It would appear, however, that these two striking individuals met only casually. Both the Martin brothers became strong supporters of Wright, and Darwin is remembered affectionately in the *Autobiography*. It seems probable that the buggy ride simply crystallized an idea which had been floating around for some time.

W. E. Martin was the owner of the E-Z Polish Company of Chicago, a firm which made polishes for shoes, stoves, and various other items. Like so many of Wright's key clients, he had an inventive turn of mind. He patented a method of printing colors on tin cans and also designed a primitive system of traffic controls. He was conscious of the need for such a system, since, like the Winslow brothers, he drove a Stanley Steamer. Steam automobiles would seem to have been quite popular in the Chicago suburbs at the turn of the century. As might be expected, he had a basement workshop where he indulged in creative puttering. His other hobby was the growing of exotic plants. In religion he was a Christian Scientist but not an active church member. In politics he was a Republican, but again, not deeply interested. His wife, on the other hand, was a Democrat and marched down Michigan Avenue as a suffragette.

In many ways Mrs. Martin seems to have been a prototype of the active clubwoman of the twentieth century. Besides campaigning for the suffrage movement, she worked hard to get Oak Park to adopt kindergarten education and ultimately succeeded in doing so. Her husband was chairman of the school board. She also raised money for various other good causes, notably the school of organic education at Fairhope, Alabama. All this, of course, was in addition to raising three children at a time when domestic conveniences were in a primitive stage. This same pattern of energy is characteristic of a good many of Wright's clients. For the most part they were active men and women, busy with all kinds of jobs outside the strictly domestic sphere. Few had independent incomes, and few were intellectuals. Only a minority were artistic, as the word is usually understood. Nonetheless, they were drawn to an architect who was undoubtedly the greatest artist that America has produced.

Ills. pp. 82–90

Mr. and Mrs. Avery Coonley (Riverside, Illinois, 1908)

More has been written about the Avery Coonleys than about any other of Wright's early clients. Grant Manson has characterized their house as "the product of that rare set of factors in architectural history, a liberal client, a great designer, and perfect trust between the two." [5] With much justification he calls it "the palazzo among prairie houses" and comments accurately on the superb air of moneyed ease which it conveys. It has been used as an illustration more than any of the other early dwellings except the Robie House; as recently as November 1955, it was again sumptuously published in *House Beautiful* magazine. How did this remarkable structure come to be built?

From all accounts Mr. and Mrs. Avery Coonley were a sophisticated, charming, and progressive couple. He was born in Rochester, New York, in 1870. His father was a lawyer who practiced in Aurora, New York, and St. Louis. His mother was the heiress to a fortune derived from the manufacturing of farm machinery; as Lydia Avery Coonley Ward she is prominent in the social history of Chicago for her sponsorship of one of the city's important salons. She was apparently a really gifted hostess. After graduating from Harvard College in 1894, Avery Coonley took graduate work at MIT, and then for a short time worked for one of the family concerns, the Chicago

82

1. Avery Coonley, courtesy of Chicago *Tribune*

Malleable Iron Company. He does not, however, seem to have been attracted to business, as was his brother Prentiss. For a few years he did editorial work for *The Little Chronicle,* a weekly magazine for use in schools, and he also interested himself in certain properties in Texas, notably the Coonley Bassett Livestock Company, of Crosbyton. In addition he gave a good deal of time to civic affairs. He was a commissioner of Cook County and a member of the Riverside School Board. His true interest, however, was in the Christian Science Church. For many years he was on its publications committee for the state of Illinois, and in 1912 the Coonleys moved to Washington, where he enlarged the scope of his work.

Mrs. Coonley was the former Queene Ferry of Detroit. She came of a family long prominent in the seed business and was a Vassar graduate, one of the few wives among Wright's clients to possess a college degree. They were also exceptional in his clientele in that she took the lead in the building project. Queene Ferry Coonley was an avid architectural amateur and became convinced of the merits of Wright's work by going to exhibitions. Her husband at first wanted "something colonial," but quickly came around as a consequence of Wright's persuasive abilities and the pleadings of his wife. Quite evidently the Coonleys were determined to create a dwelling of remarkable distinction, and they certainly succeeded in doing so.

83
2. Coonley house, exterior shot, courtesy of Wayne Andrews

Concerning their meeting in 1906 or 1907 Wright himself wrote: "About this time Mr. and Mrs. Avery Coonley came to the Oak Park workshop to ask me to build them a home at Riverside, Illinois. Unknown to me they had gone to see nearly everything they could learn I had done before coming. The day they finally came into the Oak Park workshop Mrs. Coonley said they had come because it seemed to them they saw in my houses 'the countenance of principle.' This was to me a great and sincere compliment. So I put the best in me into the Coonley house. I feel now, looking back upon it, that building was the best I could do then in the way of a house." [6] It might be added that the Coonleys completed their architectural gem by retaining Jens Jensen, the noted Chicago landscape architect, to do the grounds. They could hardly have gone further.

On close inspection the life-style of the Coonleys appears as aristocratic rather than middle-class. Mr. Coonley played tennis and enjoyed horseback riding; he disapproved of golf. His wife amused herself by doing handicraft, especially bookbinding, weaving, and knitting. She did not sew. Like the Winslows, the Moores, and the Thomases, the Coonleys were a musical family. She played the piano, he the violin. In addition, Mr. Coonley used to write nonsense poetry for family entertainment and belonged to a literary society. Both enjoyed travel, though Mr. Coonley's position as publicist for the Christian

84
3. Coonley house, exterior, courtesy of Wayne Andrews

Science Church kept him fairly close to Chicago. Mrs. Coonley was a Christian Science practitioner, and one of her requirements was that Wright work out an arrangement whereby the incoming patients would not see the outgoing ones. A double stairway took care of this matter. She was also much interested in progressive education. Both of the Coonleys considered themselves liberal or progressive politically. They admired Theodore Roosevelt and would have voted for Woodrow Wilson if they hadn't moved to Washington, where suffrage restrictions precluded it.

The Coonleys' house presents one generally unnoticed paradox. Almost any visitor would assume that its large, superbly modulated spaces were intended for entertainments on a lavish scale. The fact of the matter is that the house was decidedly a family-centered structure. The Coonleys entertained very seldom, and then only for relatives and close friends. In this respect, then, Wright went beyond the program that was given to him. One is tempted to conclude that he intuitively sensed the pleasure which these particular clients would take in this kind of environment. "We get the impression," writes Manson, "that the Coonley family had a sensitive pleasure in their Prairie House which went beyond the norm, and the spirit of their appreciation of all its features was ever strong." [7] It is significant that the family remained on excellent

85

4. Coonley house, garden elevation, courtesy of Chicago Architectural Photographing Co.

terms with Wright after the completion of the house, and in 1912 built a playhouse by him on their estate. This, too, was a building of great distinction. Perhaps Wright was justified in his liberal interpretation of the program.

Mr. and Mrs. Meyer May (Grand Rapids, Michigan, 1909)
Meyer May was born in 1873 in Rock Island, Illinois, where his father was engaged in the wholesale and retail china trade. Ten years later he moved to Grand Rapids, Michigan, when the elder May founded a men's clothing store in the city. A. May and Sons has not changed its name and still remains at its original location, one of the town's most respected establishments.

After graduating from Grand Rapids Central High School in 1890, May went on to the University of Michigan. He was, however, able to spend only two years there, since a crisis arose in 1892 when two department managers left the family firm to start their own concern. May went home to help out, quickly assumed executive status, and remained at the head of the company until his death in 1936. This early entrance into business was probably fortunate, for Meyer May turned out to be a merchandising genius. Under his guidance A. May and Sons took a leading place among the clothing stores in its part of the country. It was the first clothing store in the nation

86
5. Coonley house, first-floor plan, courtesy of Henry-Russell Hitchcock

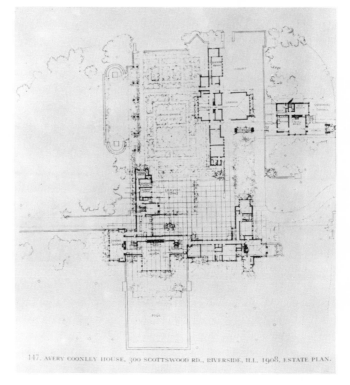

147. AVERY COONLEY HOUSE, 300 SCOTTSWOOD RD., RIVERSIDE, ILL. 1908, ESTATE PLAN.

to have showcases built for its goods, and when they were installed, clothiers from all over the Midwest came to Grand Rapids to inspect them. May was, in fact, an innovator in every phase of the clothing business. He invented the swiveling coat rack, now common in all men's clothing stores, and with his accountant and business adviser, Mr. Frank E. Seidman, he worked out an entirely new system of bookkeeping which is still used today in many department stores.

The mind behind these inventions displayed a profound respect for innovation in all fields. It was thus natural for him to hire Frank Lloyd Wright to design the backdrops for his window displays and also to do his house in 1909. How he heard of Wright is not known, but since he was a great reader, it wouldn't have been surprising if he had run across a mention of his name in a newspaper or magazine article. In any event, the two men became good friends. May was entirely happy with the house, and in later years was often instrumental in getting Wright to speak in Grand Rapids. In their relationship we sense the response of one innovating individual to another.

In addition to his connection with A. May and Sons, Meyer May was interested in the Grand Rapids Mutual Building and Loan Association and the Imperial Furniture Company. An extremely sociable individual, he was a member of the Highland Country Club and of the local Elks lodge. While not partic-

87
6. Coonley house, living room, courtesy of Chicago Architectural Photographing Co.

ularly active in synagogue affairs, he was a member in good standing of Temple Immanuel; a close associate recalls he always subscribed an appropriate pledge for its support. It might be noted here that the Mays and their in-laws, the Ambergs, were almost the only Jewish clients of Wright during his early period. The prominent families in the Chicago Jewish community, such as the Florsheims, the Kuppenheimers, and the Bensingers (of Brunswick, Balke, Collender), employed other architects. Wright's famous Jewish patrons like the Kaufmanns and the Guggenheims appeared at a much later period in his life. So enamored was Meyer May of Wright's architecture that he persuaded his father-in-law, David Amberg, to build a Wright house only a few blocks from his own dwelling.

Aside from entertaining, of which he did a great deal, May's major avocations were cards, golf, and fishing. He took great pleasure in his summer house at Charlevoix on Lake Michigan, and also enjoyed deep-sea fishing in Florida. Information on his politics is scanty, but he seems to have been an admirer of Theodore Roosevelt. His in-laws, the Ambergs, were among the few staunch Democrats to be found on the list of Wright's prairie house clients. While May was intensely interested in his house and took the lead in furnishing it, he had no such instinct for invention as Herman Winslow or W. E. Martin. His sense of innovation was felt in other directions. An anecdote

7. Coonley house, upstairs hallway, courtesy of Chicago Architectural Photographing Co.

told by an old friend is characteristic: One day while Meyer May was smoking a Lucky Strike cigarette, he noticed that the tobacco had the appearance of being toasted. He promptly wrote the American Tobacco Company and told them that they should advertise this quality. A few days later a representative of the corporation came to the city and paid him $100 for his suggestion. To this day the Lucky Strike pack says "It's Toasted."

Mr. and Mrs. Frank Thomas (Oak Park, Illinois, 1901)

Born in the little town of Point Pleasant, Ohio, in 1870, Frank Thomas moved to Chicago at an early age. After graduating from the West Division High School, his first job was with the American Exchange National Bank of Chicago. A few years later he joined A. O. Slaughter & Company, a conservative firm of stockbrokers, becoming a partner in 1903. At his retirement he was senior partner, and in keeping with his position, a member of the Chicago Stock Exchange and the Board of Trade. In addition to these organizations he belonged to the Art Institute and the Field Museum; there is no indication of much activity in either institution. In politics both husband and wife were conventional Republicans, and Mrs. Thomas worked for woman suffrage, even marching in one of the numerous suffragette parades of the period. In religion the

89
8. Coonley house, upstairs hallway, courtesy of Chicago Architectural Photographing Co.

family were faithful Episcopalians. Both Mr. Thomas and his father were vestrymen and then wardens of Grace Episcopal Church. Mrs. Thomas served and baked for church bazaars and various other functions.

Aside from the church, the leisure-time activities of the Thomas family seem to have focused on sports and music. Mr. Thomas played a good game of golf, first at the old Westward Ho Club, and later at the Oak Park Country Club, which he helped to found. Moreover, they were members of the River Forest Tennis Club, and Mrs. Thomas belonged to the Women's Athletic Club. Both of them loved music. Mrs. Thomas studied the violin in Germany as a girl, but did not keep in practice after her marriage. She also studied writing at the Lewis Institute in Chicago, and all her life was fond of poetry, including the newer forms such as free verse. All of this, of course, was in addition to bringing up two children and staging the usual round of family parties. Like the Heurtleys and the Moores, who were good friends, the Thomases were not in the least indolent or easygoing.

The relationship with Wright seems generally to have been harmonious. His choice as architect for their house was dictated by his proximity in Oak Park and "justified by his unusual ability" (Mrs. O. C. Doering, daughter of Frank Thomas). It is probable that the strongest voice in his selection was that

90
9. Coonley house, dining room, courtesy of Chicago Architectural Photographing Co.

of the aesthetically oriented Mrs. Thomas, but he also worked closely with Mr. Thomas and his father-in-law, James C. Rogers. As was his custom, Wright built in several settees and designed some pieces of furniture, which were executed in Chicago. These were heavy, massive things and not particularly comfortable, so they were soon replaced by more traditional styles. In other respects his services were thoroughly satisfactory. The family lived in the house for at least twenty-five years after its construction; certainly this is evidence of a deep attachment.

Edward Carson Waller, River Forest, Illinois.

Of all Wright's early clients Edward C. Waller was most closely connected with the inner power structure of the Chicago business world. Born in Maysville, Kentucky, in 1845, he came to Chicago with his family in 1860, and in 1866, after an initial experience in the grocery business, founded a real estate firm, which he directed actively until his final illness began in the summer of 1930. Waller specialized in downtown real estate, a line of work which brought him into contact with most of the city's financial barons, political spoilsmen, and leading architects. He was the founder and president of the Central Safety Deposit Company, which built William Le Baron Jenney's Home Insurance Company building. This structure, it will be remembered, was partially framed in iron and steel and is usually named as the first true skyscraper. For the Central Safety Deposit Company he also promoted The Rookery, one of the masterpieces of Burnham and Root. Along with Owen Aldis, who put up the Monadnock, Waller can be classed as one of the great creative patrons of the first Chicago school. In addition to real estate interests, he was also president of the North American Accident Insurance Company. If any of Wright's clients was close to the city's business elite, it was Edward Waller.

Wright first made Waller's acquaintance through the Winslows. The Winslow house had been built on Auvergne Place in River Forest directly across from the Waller home. The two families were good friends, and the Wallers admired the daring new structure enormously. In 1939 Mrs. Waller, who had lived across from it for almost half a century, told an interviewer that she never grew tired of looking at it. One consequence of this admiration was that Wright became almost a member of the Waller family circle; his participation in their Christmas parties is recounted elsewhere in this book. Another result was a continuing series of commissions from Waller and his connections. In 1895 Wright designed the Francisco Terrace apartment house for Waller in Chicago, and in 1899 a new house for the River Forest property, which was, unhappily, never built. He did, however, remodel the Waller dining room and built the handsome octagon described by John Lloyd Wright. In 1905 Waller obtained for Wright the opportunity to remodel the lobby of John Root's Rookery Building. This was important as a kind of showcase for Wright's decorative talents in the Chicago Loop. A series of multiple-housing schemes for Waller and his son Edward, Jr., kept the Wright office busy intermittently from 1901 to 1909; attention was also given during this period to plans for the further subdivision of the family property in River Forest. For this project Wright designed three houses with variants to be built speculatively; although none was ever constructed, these schemes were, as Grant Manson has pointed out, very influential on Walter Burley Griffin and John Van Bergen.

Nor was this the end of the patronage from the Waller family and its connections. Robert Roloson, whose son married Waller's daughter in 1894, commissioned four-party wall houses for his property on the south side of Chicago. He was a successful grain merchant who began his business career in the packing industry during the early eighteen seventies and ultimately became a member of the Board of Trade and Stock Exchange and director of the Diamond Match Company. Even more significant was the commission from Waller's son, "Young Ed," for the Midway Gardens in 1913. Now destroyed, this famous structure was undoubtedly one of the real master-works of the architect's career. The complete record of Wright's patronage by the Waller family is extremely impressive. It can, in fact, hardly be matched in the entire history of the Modern Movement. When to it is added the story of Waller's introduction of Wright to Daniel Burnham and the latter's amazing offer to finance six years of foreign study for Wright on condition that he would adopt the fashionable classical idiom, Waller's character takes on an even greater interest. This offer, which Manson rightly calls "a truly Medicean gesture," was made in 1894; Burnham was Waller's good friend and certainly an "establishment architect," if there was such a thing in the Chicago of that day. Wright's account of his meeting with Waller and Burnham is well known; he relates that after his refusal there was an incredulous silence in the room. What is *not usually* noticed is that Wright and Waller continued to be on good terms long after the interview. Waller probably thought at the time that his young protégé was crazy, but he did not let his opinion interfere with his continued patronage. A small man might have withdrawn his help at that point.

What manner of man was Edward Waller? He was evidently a person of commanding physical presence. Wright himself wrote that "he was the handsomest and most aristocratic individual I had ever seen." [8] He was also a man of great force of character. A biographical notice remarked, "He was a determined man and during his life in Chicago and River Forest was a power to be reckoned with. It was his policy that preserved such a large part of River Forest to become one of the most notable residential districts of the Chicago suburbs." [9] In addition to his city and suburban properties, Waller owned a summer place at Charlevoix, Michigan, and here he was a strong proponent of reforestation. He replanted several hundred acres with pine trees. Except for his outstanding abilities, there appears to have been very little to distinguish him from his fellow businessmen. He was a member of the customary clubs — the Union League, the Saddle and Cycle, and the Oak Park Country Club. His favorite recreation was golf, though a membership in the Art Institute suggests that he was perhaps more interested in art than most of his contemporaries. His family was also somewhat larger than that of most of Wright's clients; he was married twice and had seven children. Within Wright's practice Waller represents a remarkable continuation of the daring type of client who built the great commercial structures of the eighties and nineties.

Ills. pp. 96–99

Mr. and Mrs. Arthur Heurtley (Oak Park, Illinois, 1902)

By common consent the Heurtley house of 1902 is one of the gems among the prairie houses. With its almost classic repose and exquisite proportions, it suggests that the owners must have been at peace with themselves and with the world. As so frequently with Wright, one encounters paradox. The Heurtleys must have been among the least contented of the couples for whom Wright built.

Arthur Heurtley was born in Boston in 1860 and educated at a private school in Newburgh, New York, from 1864 to 1868, in the public schools of Chicago from 1868 to 1872, and at Peekskill (New York) Military Academy from 1873 to 1876. Upon his graduation from Peekskill, he entered the service of the National Park Bank of New York, remaining with that institution until 1881, in which year he moved to Chicago and joined the Merchants Loan and Trust Company. He became affiliated with the Northern Trust Company of Chicago at the time of its organization in 1889, was appointed assistant secretary in 1890 and secretary a year later. He remained with the Northern Trust until his retirement. His major achievement as a banker was in bringing some of the Marshall Field business to the Northern Trust. On the surface his career appears to have been successful. In actuality he suffered a major disappointment when the presidency, on which he had set his

96

1. Arthur Heurtley, photograph courtesy of Moffett Studio

heart, went to another candidate. In point of fact, his ambition was thoroughly unrealistic, since the presidency was at that time a hereditary possession of the Byron L. Smith family, which had founded the firm. This episode occurred when Heurtley was in his late fifties. His health broke, and he never was able to work again. He died at his country house in Muscatine, Iowa, in 1934.

The Heurtley marriage seems to have been one of those held together by social pressure. One suspects that his wife, the former Grace Crampton, was primarily a homebody. She was an expert cook and needlewoman of professional caliber. No other interests are recorded. Arthur Heurtley, on the other hand, was apparently an extremely gregarious individual. His obituary remarks that until incapacitated by illness he was an active member of the Cliff Dwellers and the Chicago and Union League Clubs, the Apollo Musical Society, of which he was president for nine years, the Chicago Golf Club of Wheaton, and the Oak Park Country Club. In addition, he was at one time or another a member of the Caxton (a group of bibliophiles), the Quadrangle at the University of Chicago, and the River Forest Tennis Club. He was also prominent in the organization of the "Les Cheneaux Club," a vacation resort on an island off Marquette, Michigan, for which Wright did a building in 1902. Not surprisingly, the Heurtleys entertained a

97
2. Heurtley house, street elevation, courtesy of Wayne Andrews

good deal, though parties must have been a strain for Mrs. Heurtley.

Heurtley's main recreation was music. He enjoyed choral singing himself and was an avid concertgoer. His son was compelled to sing in the choir of the local Episcopal church for many years, and perhaps as a consequence grew up believing in no creed. Unhappily, Mrs. Heurtley did not know one note from another and hence could not share this enthusiasm with her husband. There are also a good many other suggestions of friction within this marriage. While the house looked as tranquil as could be, the people inside it were not at all contented.

Ills. pp. 100–107

Mr. and Mrs. William Greene (Aurora, Illinois, 1912)

William Greene was born in Lisle, Illinois, in 1886 and graduated from the University of Illinois in 1908 with a degree in mechanical engineering. As the accompanying interview indicates, he first encountered the work of Frank Lloyd Wright as an undergraduate through the agency of Harry Robinson, a friend who had gone to work for Wright. What the interview does not make clear is the fascinating story of Greene's own business career. After a few years of experience with conveyor machinery, he formed a partnership in 1916 which eventually became the Barber-Greene Company, at present the world's

98

3. Heurtley house, ground-floor plan and upper-floor plan, courtesy of Henry-Russell Hitchcock

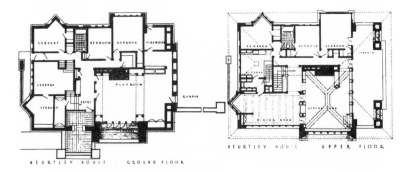

largest manufacturer of asphalt paving machines. At first the company was concerned with devices for the handling of concrete aggregate; then, when road building fell off during the Depression years, they switched over to the asphalt field, "because it looked like a coming thing." The company became the largest supplier of this type of machine to the armed forces during the Second World War. Barber-Greene machinery built roads and airfields all over the world during that conflict. Today Mr. Greene is still active in the business, but his two sons have taken over major responsibilities.

As to his political and social outlook, Mr. Greene has always been a Republican, but has favored the income tax, popular election of senators, child labor laws, the direct primary—in fact, all progressive legislation which leads to a better spread of opportunity. "Other manufacturers," he remarks, "have always found us a bit too liberal politically." His hobbies are golf and photography, and the Greenes have been able to do a good bit of world traveling for business and pleasure. The Barber-Greene Company has plants in several countries. For several years Greene has run two model farms at Lisle, Illinois, and he has donated a good deal of land to the Girl Scouts of America, which is his favorite charity. In his childhood he was a member of the Episcopal Church, but discontinued his affiliation in later life.

99
4. Heurtley house, living room, courtesy of Grant Manson

Today, the house is occupied by Greene's elder son. The Greenes themselves live in a small one-story dwelling on an adjoining lot. A few years ago Mrs. Greene had a heart attack, and a move became necessary. Unhappily the construction of this second house destroyed most of the landscaping, which was the work of the famous Chicago landscape architect Jens Jensen, who also landscaped Wright's Coonley House. A comparison of the present structure with Wright's rendering of 1912 will show that certain additions were made as the Greene family grew larger. These, however, were very much in keeping with the feeling of the original work. The following interview with Mr. and Mrs. Greene took place August 8, 1964.

Mr. Greene–Mr. Eaton   August 8, 1964

Interviewer:
Can you tell me when you first got interested in Mr. Wright?
Greene:
Well, it was maybe about 1907. I had some friends at the University from Oak Park who knew his family and knew his work and during the last years at the University we were planning a new fraternity building and one of the members a couple of years ahead of us had gone with Mr. Wright, and through that connection he got Mr. Wright to submit a proposed drawing to the fraternity and I was one of the few of the group that was

100
1. Mr. and Mrs. Greene, courtesy of Richard Nickel

quite delighted with the proposed drawing; also I happened to be head of the chapter at the time.

Interviewer:

What did you like about it?

Greene:

I don't know. The lines seemed to be pleasing. Well, neither one of us, my wife or myself, was strongly traditional. We had a general attitude at that time of trying not to be too influenced by what had gone before and the lines just seemed pleasing to us. The difficulty in selling it to a group like that was that the head of the school of architecture at Illinois was a member of the fraternity and the boys looked to him for leadership and he did not countenance anyone as new and radical as Frank Lloyd Wright. As a matter of fact, the boys used that drawing for two or three years in their rushing. They said that this is the building we hope to build, and some of the men that followed me who were there when the final decision was made were very disappointed that the decision was made to use more of a conventional architect and a more conventional-type building.

Interviewer:

And then in 1912 when you decided to build your own house, you went to Mr. Wright?

Greene:

Yes!

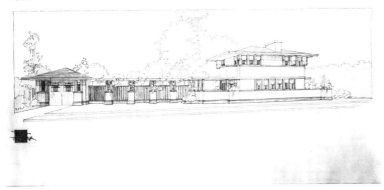

2. Rendering of Greene house by Frank Lloyd Wright studio

Interviewer:

Do you recall the circumstances of your first interview with him?

Greene:

Well, as I say, our main discussions were with Harry Robinson and when we visited Wright's office (his office was in the Fine Arts Building), we were certainly low-income bracket at the time. We were rather ambitious to want to build a house at all, but we decided that we would certainly like to study the possibility of a Wright design if we did anything, so we went there with no feeling of assurance that we were going to use him, and they submitted quite a variety of sketches as well as showing us drawings of some of the other houses they had done, including the Avery Coonley, which they had just finished, and the Avery Coonley School in Downer's Grove.

Mrs. Greene:

It was the Avery Coonley School.

Greene:

But those, of course, were way beyond us. We had to have a small house and a very inexpensive house, and as Wright said, our needs were below anything that he had done then, but they were intrigued with the idea of working on a smaller house so they just started the study of working from our lot. We just had a corner fifty-foot lot at the time; we didn't have this area. We

102
3. Greene house, front elevation, courtesy of Richard Nickel

acquired two additional lots later, and so they were limiting themselves to the one corner lot. The features that were not generally accepted then were to have the living quarters over-looking the garden and putting the kitchen up front.

Interviewer:

Do you recall what your requirements in a house were, Mrs. Greene?

Mrs. Greene:

Well, we had one bath and four bedrooms; we would sit on our porch and hear people in automobiles exclaiming over the house, saying "Do you know they have the kitchen in the front?" That seemed to be astounding them.

Interviewer:

But you were happy to have the kitchen up front?

Mrs. Greene:

Oh, yes, we liked it and we found the house convenient, liva-ble. It wasn't until our third child came that we felt the need of more room. Then we put the addition on. It was a practical, good house.

Greene:

The fireplace was, of course, one of the first requirements and that also would have been one of Wright's first specifications for a house.

EAST

WEST

0   5   10   15

103
4. Green house, east-west eleva-tion, redrawn from original print by Thomas Snodgrass

Interviewer:
You knew already that he always wanted a fireplace whenever possible?

Greene:
I'm not sure whether we knew that in advance or not.

Interviewer:
Did you find him personally a pleasant individual to deal with?

Greene:
Yes. The range of choice was surprising. We didn't have anything forced on us. There was a question of what our needs were and then trying to study how to meet those needs and possibilities. If we had been wealthy, I don't doubt he would have given us the works as he did other clients, and try to oversell which wouldn't have been good business for him to get us to take a large house. This had to be simple, had to be boiled down to fairly simple living requirements.

Interviewer:
Did you have any special requirements beyond the four bedrooms, the bath and the kitchen?

Greene:
Well, the fireplace was the main thing and we wanted a screened porch.

Mrs. Greene:
We had liked the wide eaves and the windows opening out. We

104
5. Greene house, north-south elevation, redrawn from original print by Thomas Snodgrass

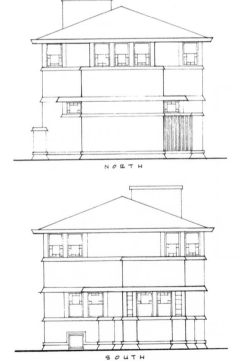

NORTH

SOUTH

0   5   10   15

never had rain come in our house. It was very nice with those wide eaves.

Greene:

Well, of course, the casement windows were a trademark of his and we were rather skeptical. At least we had quite a study and quite a discussion. Also the question was up whether to have the windows open in or out, and his out-opening casement windows were somewhat of a Wright innovation and with the type of adjustment we were able to get, we have since found that they were practical.

Interviewer:

What kind of heating did he recommend?

Mrs. Greene:

It was always hot air.

Greene:

It was hot air heating, coal fired, of course; central furnace. That was a very difficult thing to put in, too, with his layout. He didn't have the normal walls going up to the ceiling so we did have some difficulty and as a matter of fact our first heating plant was never too successful in heating all of the upstairs rooms.

Interviewer:

You changed that at some later date?

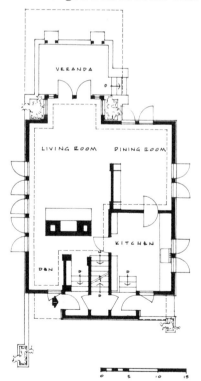

105
6. Greene house, ground-floor plan, redrawn from original print by Thomas Snodgrass

Mrs. Greene:
We enlarged the house; then we put in hot-water heating.
Greene:
And that was much more satisfactory, and we could get the pipes to the upstairs radiators without any problems, but before we couldn't get our warm air ducts up. Well, breaks in the ducts retarded the flow. Of course, at that time they didn't have forced air heating. It was all gravity flow.
Mrs. Greene:
There was a little balcony at the back at the corner there on the original house and that was a very nice feature too with a French door opening onto it.
Interviewer:
You sound as if you had taken a very close personal interest in the construction of the house, which I would expect from an engineer.
Mrs. Greene:
My husband could have been an architect, and a good one. He was very good at it and he had a big hand in designing this house.
Greene:
Well, we literally, mentally lived in the house. Of course, we had cut-outs of the furniture, and studied our closet needs very carefully. Some of the closet areas could be used that they

106
7. Greene house, second-story plan, redrawn from original print by Thomas Snodgrass

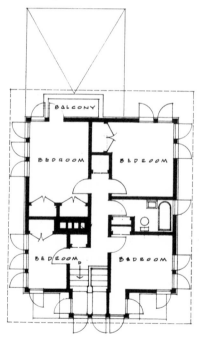

hadn't suggested, such as that little cupboard on the stairway. There was unused space, but with that kind of mentally living in it, we ended up with something that was completely practical for our needs and for years we couldn't see anything that we would change about it. I think we became rather snobbish about it.

Interviewer:

Well, it seems to me you had every reason to. It's a handsome building and evidently fulfilled your needs very nicely. Did you find your business transactions with Mr. Wright quite satisfactory?

Greene:

Yes.

Interviewer:

You mentioned earlier that he himself was having a difficult time paying his bills.

Greene:

Well, we were able to pay his fee on schedule so there was no reason for any trouble and his specifications were very carefully worked out. They were worked out in good detail and we were fortunate to have a builder that was also interested in his architecture and who was wanting to do a good job.

Interviewer:

Who was your builder?

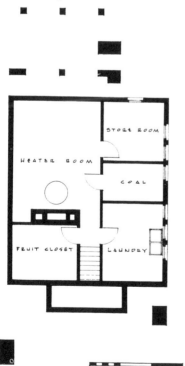

107

8. Greene house, basement plan, redrawn from original print by Thomas Snodgrass

Greene:

His name was Sylvester. He, I am afraid, is not living now and as a matter of fact he wasn't in Aurora for too long after that, but he took it as somewhat a challenge, and I think was very careful about the concrete footings — particularly about getting very adequate footing under the chimney. The fact that there was never a crack in the plaster where the chimney went up through the ceiling was pretty good evidence that we had a good foundation. When we came to our porch, it wasn't excavated; it was set on footings, and there was some settlement in the porch, which we had to have shored up later.

Interviewer:

And your contractor had good masons and carpenters and so on working for him?

Greene:

Yes, very good. You see, well, that woodwork was very elaborate. The mitering of those joints in the trim was virtually millwork done on the job. I don't think we could get anything like that now, and if we could, it would be very costly.

Interviewer:

Did Mr. Wright build in some furniture for you?

Greene:

Yes, the buffet that was incorporated into the divider between the dining room and the living room. As a matter of fact, it's still over in the basement of the old house, and that what we had to take out when we enlarged the house.

Mrs. Greene:

We have the dining room table and chairs and davenport that he designed.

Interviewer:

Have you found them to be comfortable and workable pieces of furniture?

Mrs. Greene:

Not the dining room chairs; they are not for lounging certainly.

Greene:

I think they're the only good pieces of furniture that Wright made. So many of his pieces of furniture were uncomfortable as chairs, and I think our design has generally been both comfortable and pleasing as furniture.

Interviewer:

You mentioned that you had visited at one time or another some of his other big jobs, and had called on him at Taliesin East and West.

Greene:

Well, yes, I remember one time at Taliesin East we called on him when we were facing a maintenance job. This plaster is on lath which was preferred at that time to plaster on metal lath.

109

That was one of the things Wright insisted on as better construction and it has proved to be. But we've washed over the plaster with a cement type of finish at different times to fill up the hair cracks. There's been no bad cracking or bad settling, but from time to time it did need a wash coat and we would also do the wood with a creosote stain. And at one time we were wondering about some other color than our buff and wanted to ask his advice about it. What was his comment on it?

Mrs. Greene:

Well, I know he didn't like what we suggested, so we kept to the old buff.

Greene:

Well, he said, why do you want to change anyway? I have trouble keeping my people from making changes. Why not take what I gave you and live with it? We said to him, well you're doing nothing but change yourself, how do you reconcile that? Of course he was building all the time.

Interviewer:

Do you feel that your own engineering training helped you to get along with Mr. Wright or to be sympathetic to him?

Greene:

Well, I don't know. Yes, it certainly helped us to get along with

110
1. E. E. Boynton, courtesy of Mrs. B. L. Boynton

him and also helped us to keep our construction sound. I don't know that it had any connection with our being in sympathy with his artistic ability. I guess that was something else.

Interviewer:

Are there any comments that you'd like to make about the job Mr. Wright did for you or your relationship with him, Mrs. Greene?

Mrs. Greene:

Oh, everything was satisfactory I think. We liked him, liked his personality.

Interviewer:

He was supposed to be a man of great personal charm.

Mrs. Greene:

Yes, we liked him. We certainly never regret building our house.

Edward E. and Beulah Boynton (Rochester, New York, 1907)

Ills. pp. 110–117

The personal life of Edward Everett Boynton was dogged by tragedy. His wife, whom he loved deeply, died in 1900, and he also lost two sons in early childhood. He never remarried, and his later life was devoted to the happiness and well-being of his only daughter, Beulah, who was born in 1886, and for whom he built a house by Frank Lloyd Wright in 1907–1909.

111
2. Boynton house, street elevation, courtesy of Wayne Andrews

Born in 1857, Edward Boynton was an excellent example of the successful American businessman-salesman. At first a salesman and later a partner in the Ham Lantern Company of Rochester, New York, he remained with the firm after its absorption in 1908 by the giant trust of the lantern industry, the R. E. Dietz Company of Chicago. Boynton's persuasive and engaging personality enabled him, his daughter remarks, "to sell more lanterns than any other man in the world." For some time he was able to work only three months of every year, as he managed to saturate the market within that given period. Like Diamond Jim Brady, Boynton was one of those businessmen whose basic talent was for selling.

While business frequently called him to Chicago and New York, both Boynton and his daughter wanted to settle in Rochester. Boynton first heard of Wright through Warren MacArthur, his business partner in the Ham Lantern Company. MacArthur, for whom Wright had built one of his earliest houses in the Kenwood district of Chicago (1892), was an enthusiast, and he evidently converted both Boynton and his daughter. The latter seems to have resembled Mrs. Avery Coonley in that she had a considerable interest in architectural design. After momentary hesitation in choosing between Wright and Claude Bragdon (Rochester's leading modern architect), the Boyntons settled on Wright.

112
3. Boynton house, rear elevation with pool, courtesy of Nathan R. Graves

Today Beulah Boynton recalls that Wright was "extremely good-looking, had a keen sense of humor, and a light in his blue eyes." She found him very pleasant and not at all temperamental. Obviously they got along well together, and he was receptive to a number of suggestions from her. These included continuous cove moldings to aid in cleaning, six-foot-wide drawers on ball bearings in her bedroom to provide full-length storage of fragile dresses, a false floor in the basement to elevate steamer trunks and prevent mildew, and adjustable backs on the Wright-designed dining and lounge chairs. In contradistinction to most of the architect's clients, she maintains that these were very comfortable. Evidently she became quite interested in the process of construction, since she learned to read both working drawings and specifications while the house was being built.

Economically the Boyntons belonged among the more affluent of Wright's clients. Without possessing the wealth of the Coonleys or Darwin Martins, they were very comfortably situated. The cost of the house and lot together was $55,000, a large sum for 1908. Wright participated in the choice of the somewhat hilly site and insisted on the expensive addition of twenty-eight elm trees. In numerous other respects he also exercised a remarkably complete control over the job. All of the furniture was designed expressly for the house and built

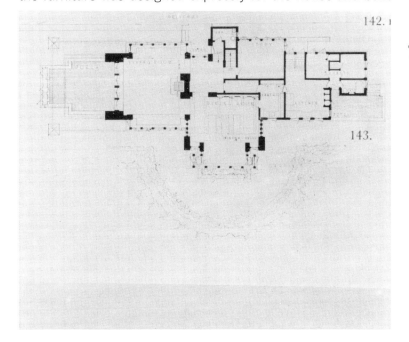

142.

143.

113

4. Boynton house,
first-floor plan,
courtesy of Henry-
Russell Hitchcock

locally. One of the most striking pieces was an elaborate dining room table with internally lit, recessed flower receptacles; along with it went custom-tailored Irish table linen to match. Much of the hardware was also of original design, and on the exterior of the house Wright used his customary extensive apparatus of window boxes, urns, and other planting devices. A thirteen-foot-wide fireplace acted as a room divider, and the front entrance was well concealed because Wright thought that "they are just like a punch in the stomach."

The house must be understood as the setting for the social activity of a successful businessman and his vivacious young daughter. After Beulah Boynton's marriage in 1908 to a New York stockbroker, she and her husband continued to live in it until 1918, when they moved to New York. The widespread use of the incandescent bulb at this time caused a decline in lantern sales, but the Boynton's financial circumstances remained extremely comfortable. The tennis court on the side lawn was the chief center for Beulah's social life, and her father found recreation in membership in several fraternal orders. These included the Genesee Falls Lodge (F&M), the Hamilton Chapter (RAM), the Monroe Commandery of the Knights Templar, the Rochester Consistory, and the Damascus Temple. Like many salesmen, Boynton was evidently a joiner. Both he and his daughter were members in good standing of

5. Boynton house, living room, courtesy of Mrs. B. L. Boynton

the Presbyterian Church, though she became an Episcopalian after her marriage. Both were Republicans but politically inactive. Aside from tennis, Beulah Boynton's main recreations were extensive reading in historical fact and fiction and a passion for automobiles. She owned one of the first electric cars in Rochester as well as a two-cylinder Cadillac, a Stutz, and a Marmon.

Like the vast majority of Wright's other prairie house clients, the Boyntons were well satisfied with their dwelling. In a 1955 newspaper interview Beulah Boynton recalled that after they moved in (March 1908), many people asked to be shown through the house, particularly on Sundays. "People thought it was revolutionary," she remarked, "and the most frequent comment I heard was that it was a style of architecture that wouldn't last." She also said: "We particularly liked the sense of space and light in the house. There were no features about it we didn't like or found inconvenient." The reporter, obviously much taken with the house added: "Although the dining room furniture is somewhat severe and uncomfortable looking, the visitor is struck by the way it blends with the handsome, pleasantly-lit room. Impressive too, is the fireplace, built in a style that has only lately been taken up by younger modern architects." [10]

Additional light is thrown on Wright's early practice by

6. Boynton house, living room, courtesy of Mrs. B. L. Boynton

George T. Swan, son of George L. Swan of Swan and Gorseline, the firm which built the house. He frankly states that the contractors expected trouble with Wright but discovered to their surprise and delight that reasonably amicable relations with him were possible so long as they adhered exactly to his specifications and instructions. "He made no great trial for the contractors," says Swan, "but he gave the workmen fits. I was too young to have known Mr. Wright but I heard a great deal about him from my father. He became, in time, a kind of legend in our house." A year was required to build the Boynton house, and during this period Wright would often pop into town without anyone expecting him. Workmen would leave the job at night without seeing the architect on the property, and find him there when they reported for work in the morning. "He might come into town on a train that arrived at midnight," relates Mr. Swan. "He wouldn't put up at a hotel. He would hire a hack and go directly to the Boynton house and stay there the remainder of the night. He would never leave the house during his stay in Rochester, which might continue two or three days. He was on the job night and day, though, of course, no workmen were there at night. He once made one of his unexpected visits during a spell of miserable weather. It was cold and rainy. As yet there was no roof on the house. Wright had workmen throw up a sort of lean-to, a few two-by-fours with a tar-

7. Boynton house, dining room, courtesy of Mrs. B. L. Boynton

paulin flung over it, and he remained in this during the night. He seemed to feel that when he was here he had to live uninterruptedly, with his work." [11]

Wright's fame was spreading, and he might easily have been a social lion. Two of Rochester's most elegant ladies, whose practice it was to entertain distinguished men and women who visited the city, successively rode out to the building site, tiptoed through the mud, and asked Wright to be their dinner guest. His declination was gracious but firm; he could not, he said, since he had so little time in Rochester, spare a minute away from his work.

When bricks were being laid, or wooden beams were being put in place, or floorboards fitted, Wright stood over the workmen with an alert gaze looking for the most minute imperfection. Every foot of work under his inspection needed to be flawless. Bricks were taken out, replaced, fitted anew, and refitted. Like many men of genius, he was capable of taking infinite pains.

In short, we have a picture of Wright's practice which completely belies the popular belief that he was lax in supervision. Obviously, the reverse was true in the case of the Boynton house. It is unlikely that any of Wright's clients received more devoted service from him than Edward and Beulah Boynton.

117
8. Boynton house, dining room, courtesy of Mrs. B. L. Boynton

Ills. pp. 118–121

Mr. and Mrs. Eugene A. Gilmore (Madison, Wisconsin, 1908)
Of all Wright's early clients Eugene A. Gilmore probably had the greatest impact on American life in the twentieth century. While the Robies, Martins, and Coonleys are known to history only through their connection with Wright, Gilmore occupies a small but secure place of his own making. There is a certain irony in this, since he was obviously among the less affluent clients on Wright's list.

A descendant of that sturdy Protestant stock which originally populated so much of the Midwest, Eugene Allen Gilmore was born July 4, 1871, in the small town of Brownville, Nebraska. His father, a merchant and farmer, had come from Greencastle, Indiana, to try his fortune in the new country west of the Missouri. Young Gilmore resolved to get a college education and enrolled in DePauw University back in Indiana. He took with him to DePauw his typewriter, which he had learned to use in a business course, and made his expenses through college by working as secretary to the president of the university. He graduated in 1893, subsequently read law in the office of an Indianapolis attorney, and was admitted to the Indiana bar in 1895.

Ambitious for further training, he went east to attend the Harvard Law School, taking with him again his reliable Remington typewriter. He took a position in the office of the dean of

118
1. Eugene A.
Gilmore

the Law School, and his typewriter was the first officially used in that famous school. He contributed to the *Harvard Law Review* and also installed a card catalogue system to keep student records and a letterpress which greatly facilitated keeping track of the extensive school correspondence, thus displaying the legal talent and administrative energy which marked his entire career. He took his LL.B. in 1899, and after three years with a Boston law firm, he accepted an appointment in 1902 as assistant professor at the University of Wisconsin Law School, where he was to spend the next twenty years of his life.

In 1899 Gilmore married Blanche Bayse of Rockport, Indiana, whom he had met at DePauw. Their marriage proved to be exceptionally happy, and Mrs. Gilmore, a friendly and energetic person in her own right, was soon conscious that she had married someone destined for an important career. It is only fair to note here, however, that it was he who took the lead in their 1908 building project with Frank Lloyd Wright.

At Madison, Gilmore taught constitutional law and the law of partnerships and public service companies. Promoted to full professor in 1903, he served as acting dean in 1912–1913 and as president of the Association of American Law Schools in 1919–1920. He also wrote voluminously. From his pen came *Gilmore on Partnership* (1908), and he was editor of

119

2. Gilmore house, front elevation, courtesy of Carrol K. Eaton

Modern American Law (fifteen volumes, 1910–1913). In addition he was active in public affairs; he represented the state of Wisconsin in the National Conference of Commissioners on Uniform State Laws, and he assisted committees of the state legislature in drafting the Railroad Commission Law, the Public Utilities Act, and the Workmen's Compensation Act.

In 1920 Gilmore was asked to become exchange professor of law at the University of the Philippines, and a new chapter of his life began. He was both popular with the students and successful in upgrading the curriculum and reorganizing the law library, and his family liked the country and the people. He returned to the University of Wisconsin for a short time, but in 1922 was appointed Vice-Governor of the Philippines by President Harding. He held that office until 1930, serving with Governors Leonard Wood, Henry L. Stimson, and Dwight F. Davis.

In 1930, Gilmore returned to the United States to become dean of the University of Iowa Law School. In 1934, he was named president of the University of Iowa and served with distinction as head of that institution until his retirement in 1940. He then accepted a challenging "special assignment" as the first full-time dean of the University of Pittsburgh Law School to put into effect an expanding academic program for that distinguished school. World War II, however, forced the virtual

120

3. Gilmore house, front elevation, courtesy of Carrol K. Eaton

suspension of all law-school activity for its duration, and Gilmore returned to Iowa City, where he lived until his death in 1953 at the age of eighty-two.

The aspect of this career which will immediately strike any observer is Gilmore's extraordinary combination of scholarly competence and administrative talent. As a legal scholar he commanded respect, but as an administrator he was almost a genius. In some way or other he managed to improve every institution with which he came in contact. His services to Wisconsin are obvious.

In the Philippines as Vice-Governor he was secretary of the Department of Public Instruction, with its subordinate bureau of education, public health, and quarantine. Under his direction education was extended to all forty-eight provinces, 1,100,000 students were enrolled, and 25,000 teachers were employed. In his capacity as chairman of the Board of Regents of the University of the Philippines he built up that institution substantially, and he also notably improved the quality of public health personnel. And while he was doing all this, he became sufficiently knowledgeable about Indonesian customary law to serve as chairman of a committee of the subject for the American Council on Learned Societies from 1934 to 1940. Although his presidency of the University of Iowa coincided with the great Depression, he maintained its educational qual-

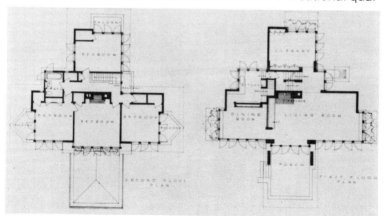

121
4. Gilmore house, ground-floor plan, second-floor plan, courtesy of Elizabeth Gilmore Holt

ity at a high level and added key faculty personnel. He even put up a number of much needed new buildings. Clearly, Gilmore was a formidable administrator if there ever was one. While not an innovator like Daniel Coit Gilman or Charles W. Eliot, he was the very type of the successful university builder.

What drew this man to Frank Lloyd Wright? With a growing family (Eugene, Jr., born in 1902, and Elizabeth in 1905), the Gilmores began to contemplate building a larger house, one which would suit their needs better than the conventional dwelling in which they were living. At the suggestion of Richard T. Ely, the famous liberal economist who was also a family friend, they bought a 120-by-200-foot lot at the top of a hill in the western section of Madison which overlooked the city and the lakes surrounding it. Professor Joseph Jastrow of the Philosophy Department was at that time in the process of remodeling his home (without professional architectural assistance), and he brought to their attention the spring 1908 issue of the *Architectural Record,* which was devoted to the work of Wright. Jastrow admired Wright's architecture immensely, and after perusing the magazine, so did the Gilmores. They engaged Wright with commendable directness. For them his appeal lay in his functional emphasis. Aware of his "Japanese influence" and "thorough and meticulous approach," they

122

hired him simply because they believed that he would give them "an attractive home of artistic design."

Mrs. Gilmore remembers Wright as "a vigorous, pleasant, intelligent man who spoke with authority." Happy with the site, he was confident that he could do a house for them within their $8000 budget and submitted his design only three weeks after his initial visit with the family. He invited Mrs. Gilmore to visit his Oak Park studio where they could discuss revisions, and she recalls being much taken with his wife and family as well as their home. She especially liked the large oak tree growing up through the entrance court. Since she did not suggest many revisions, they spent a pleasant evening listening to piano rolls. Her husband supervised the construction of the house with Wright's drawings and specifications as his guide, and since he was not able to engage a contractor, had to hire an additional carpenter, with the result that the house cost $2000 over the budget. The construction was different from anything the carpenter had known before, and the mason had difficulty with the extraordinarily wide chimney carrying three flues. Wright visited the job only three times, the last to help mix the colors for the interior rough plaster walls. The Gilmores seem, nevertheless, to have been well satisfied with his role in the construction phase of their building project.

123

The family occupied the house in late fall, 1908. Decoration was primarily Mrs. Gilmore's responsibility, but she accepted numerous suggestions from Wright. It was evidently a family-centered structure; the three children (Eugene, Jr., Elizabeth, and John A. (born 1910) enjoyed the low-scaled spaces and frolicked through the glass doors to balconies off their bedrooms. While Mr. Gilmore's major interests were his family and the law, he did a certain amount of entertaining for his academic associates and professional colleagues. "Some of these," Mrs. Gilmore admits, "thought the house a bit peculiar." Aside from their residence in a Frank Lloyd Wright house, however, the Gilmores were in no way unusual. Their recreations, for example, were quite conventional. In the winter, the Gilmores enjoyed skating on Lake Mendota and coasting on University Heights; in the summer, it was canoeing on Madison's beautiful lakes. In addition, Gilmore's biographers note that he was a tennis player, a Congregationalist, and a Republican. While Gilmore must have been a politically sensitive individual in order to make such a distinguished career, one does not have the impression that his commitment to his party was especially passionate. He knew and liked both Henry L. Stimson and "Fighting Bob" LaFollette, who were, after all, very different types of Republicans, and he was never identified with the political philosophy of either one. His interest in government appears to have been administrative, not ideological.

On the whole the Gilmores were well satisfied with their residence, which, because of its dramatic lines, is today often known as "the airplane house." Their major mistake, in Mrs. Gilmore's opinion, was in submitting to Wright's idea of a main entrance below grade. "This was low, narrow, and conducive to head-bumping." Subsequent owners have altered it by building an outside entrance stairway. A two-car garage has been added to replace the original carport, and the daring cantilevers have also required reinforcement. The Gilmores found their Wright-designed chairs uncomfortable and eventually replaced them, but continued to use the other handsome pieces. Finally Mrs. Gilmore sounds the perennial lament: insufficient closet space.

From the foregoing account it is clear that Eugene Gilmore successfully avoided the traditionalist attitudes so frequently characteristic of American lawyers. Very few representatives of the legal profession appear on the list of Wright's early clients; it may well be that the law produces a conservative outlook in its practitioners which works against architectural innovation. In his energy, ability, and general outlook on life, Gilmore greatly resembles many of the other owners of prairie houses. Like Edward Boynton, he wanted an up-to-date house

125

which would be in tune with the trend of the times, and by going to Frank Lloyd Wright he got it.

Frederick C. Robie, Chicago, Illinois (1908–1909)

Ills. pp. 126–133

Frederick C. Robie was born in Chicago in 1876, educated at the Yale School in the city and the Chicago Manual Training School, and took an engineering degree at Purdue University in 1896. On graduation he entered the employment of the Excelsior Supply Company, and in the years 1901–1909 was successively secretary, treasurer, and assistant manager of that firm; he was also president of the Excelsior Manufacturing Company, which made bicycles. In politics Mr. Robie was a Republican, and on the social side he was a member of the Chicago Athletic and Automobile Clubs and of the South Shore Country Club. The following interview between Mr. Robie and his son, which is reprinted by permission of *Architectural Forum,* for October 1958, deals in detail with the circumstances surrounding the building of the famous Robie House, one of the true classics of modern architecture.

Robie Jr.:
Father, one thing many people have been interested in for the past 40 years is what kind of house did you want in the first place?
Robie Sr.:
I definitely wanted it fireproof, and unlike the sort of thing prevalent

126
1. Robie house, street elevation, courtesy of Henry-Russell Hitchcock

in the homes of that period. The idea of most of those houses was a kind of conglomeration of architecture, on the outside, and they were absolutely cut up inside. They were drafty because they had great big stair wells, occupying a lot of valuable space, interfering with outside window gazing. I wanted no part of that. I wanted rooms without interruptions. I wanted the windows without curvature and doo-dads inside and out. I wanted all the daylight I could get in the house, but shaded enough by overhanging eaves to protect from the weather. I wanted sunlight in my living room in the morning before I went to work, and I wanted to be able to look out and down the street to my neighbors without having them invade my privacy. I certainly didn't want a lot of junk—a lot of fabrics, draperies, and what not, or old-fashioned roller shades with the brass fittings on the ends—in my line of vision, gathering dust and interfering with window washing. No sir, I didn't want any wide trim on the doorways or windows. I wanted it narrow, to bring in a wider window, to give me more light.

I wanted to have the bedroom quarters and nursery activities separate and exclusively for the use of the children, all this to be offset on the side by a master bedroom, with a fireplace. I wanted a brick wall to keep the children from wandering out of the yard and getting lost. The whole thing was so nebulous that I could not explain it to anybody.

But I finally got it on paper in various sketches, which numbered about half a dozen, and displayed them to friends of mine in the building business. These were pretty hard-headed Chicago citizens who had weathered the storm of politics in the building of structures. They looked at these things and they thought I had gone nuts.

Well, maybe so, but it was my money. They said: "No. We're not in

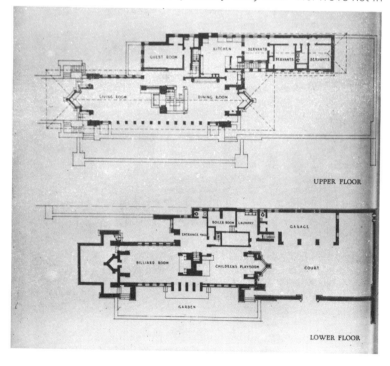

UPPER FLOOR

LOWER FLOOR

127
2. Robie house, ground-floor plan, upper-floor plan, courtesy of Henry-Russell Hitchcock

for that kind of job. We build big stuff of steel, of concrete, and all this kind of stuff—bronze elevator gates and that kind of bric-a-brac." So they were out.

Robie Jr.:

How about architects?

Robie Sr.:

And architects. I had a multiplicity of men who had been accustomed to spending large sums of money, and they had expensive ideas. I wanted a house of reasonable cost as well. I probably contacted indirectly or directly a half dozen of these men. I did a little traveling around, and ran across a constant fillip: "I know what you want, one of those damn Wright houses." It was a good advertisement for Mr. Wright. I contacted him, and from the first we had a definite community of thought. When I talked in mechanical terms, he talked and thought in architectural terms. I thought, well, he was in my world.

Robie Jr.:

Father, what year was that?

Robie Sr.:

That was, let's see, that was long about Christmastime, 1906. We agreed on a procedure. He would make sketches and submit them within a reasonable time. I told him flat I didn't expect to build immediately. Take his time—which he did, and *how*. He spent a great deal of energy and thought and time, and he became more enthusiastic about the possibilities as he was able to work out the puzzle of placing rooms.

He had some commitment on hand, but we were not in a hurry. We were very comfortable, happy, and the difference of a few months would mean nothing in our lifetime. Here was a structure that was going to last as long as we lived, we hoped. And it was going to be a

128
3. Robie house, living room, courtesy of Chicago Architectural Photographing Co.

comfortable place. It was not going to be built on in corners and what not—like telescopic arrangements of the New England homes in early times.

Robie Jr.:

Did you have any trouble in getting building permits owing to the house's unusual construction?

Robie Sr.:

In purchasing the plot, I was under a verbal obligation to build a house which would cost a minimum of about $20,000. That was well within the figure I had in mind. In about a year, we decided that we'd go ahead. By then Mr. Wright and I were in hearty accord. Practically the last detail that I, as future occupant and owner, had to attend to was to be sure that all the contracts were signed, and so on, and funds made available to the contractor who was to pay the bill. It only took probably a couple of hours, but it took a lot of thought, and I wanted to conserve my investments until the funds were probably going to be needed.

During this period, Mr. Wright had done a beautiful job of weeding out the contractors. He covered the bids with meticulous care. I was amazed. The man who finally built the house was a man by the name of Barnard & Co. He was a go-getting, two-fisted, high-spitting sort of a guy, and was a thorough mechanic in the art of household construction, having been in it from the day he was about 16. At his first job, I believe, he carried the beer to the contractor's men.

Once we began, progress went very rapidly. With practically no delay he put in the chimney, and the side walls then went up carefully. Every two or three layers of brick, in order to preserve the continuity and the long-line appearance, Mr. Barnard checked it with an instrument. There wasn't any by-guess-or-by-God business. He did a

4. Robie house, living room, courtesy of Chicago Architectural Photographing Co.

beautiful job; it developed into what I wanted, and what was satisfactory to Mr. Wright. The architect was responsible for that, and he took his responsibility very seriously. I know he was often on the job bright and early in the morning and stayed as long as he and Mr. Barnard wanted to settle things. The plans were so perfect that Barnard afterward told me he might as well have been making a piece of machinery.

It wasn't long before we were under cover. I went away on a business trip and came back and found the roof on, the walls up, and they were getting ready to cover the concrete floors with wood. And a beautiful job they did of that. Of course you could get wood in those days that is pretty difficult to get today.

There was some experimentation in the house; the building of indirect lighting around the side walls of the living room, for example, and the introduction of indirect heating by having the radiators strung along in the floor in front of doorways and windows with the pipes actually below the floor, which helped warm up the slabs, so that there was no shock of stepping on the cold floor, particularly in the bedrooms.

I had very little participation in these details. That was Mr. Wright's job. Then, all of a sudden, one day he said: "I have brought Mr. Mitchell along with me to have a little conference with you. Now I have got a commitment to go to Tokyo, Japan, and do a job over there, building a small hotel that won't fall down with the next shiver of the land. Mr. Mitchell will carry on the job and report direct to you as may be necessary. And if he can get along with you as well as I can, and he has with me, I think probably you and he can team up pretty well."

My last visit with Mr. Wright was that day he and Mitchell and I

130
5. Robie house, dining room, courtesy of William Hasbrouck

were together. It happened to occur to me, although Mr. Wright had not mentioned it, that a final payment might as well be settled. Even at that point, every single detail had worked out commercially and practically as we had anticipated and hoped.

Relationships with Mr. Wright were ideal. It seems inconceivable that the foresight, the knowledge, and the intense desire to do just the right thing could have been imbedded in a man like him — possibly it was in his hair — remember, it was kind of long.

Robie Jr.:
Were there any extras on the job?

Robie Sr.:
None. The actual total cost of the house proper, including all items — even interest and taxes, was $35,000. The cost of the lot was $14,000. Special furnishings, such as a hand-woven rug from Austria, which were provided under Mr. Wright's direction, came to about $10,000.

Robie Jr.:
So your total cost was about?

Robie Sr.:
$59,000.

Robie Jr.:
And the budget you had set up in your mind was what?

Robie Sr.:
$60,000. It was one of the cleanest business deals I ever had.

Robie Jr.:
So there you have a few of my father's memories. My own childhood memories are rather vivid. For example, I remember visits to the huge sand pile used to make mortar, and walking on the catwalks that were used to wheelbarrow materials to the house. Then later from our raised living room and dining room, we could look out over

131
6. Robie house, children's playroom, courtesy of William Hasbrouck

a two-block vacant area to the Midway Plaisance. At that time the central portion of the Midway was flooded in wintertime, and we could watch people skating there.

Still later, after father sold the house, and we moved away, I came back to attend the University of Chicago, and my fraternity house was only a block away. Very quickly I heard weird stories about my old home. One that I remember was that it had been built by a retired sea captain and his wife, to resemble an ocean liner, with its long deck-like balconies on the south and west. Supposedly the captain and his wife were buried in the vault below the front porch—really a storage area we had used as a wine cellar. There were other wild stories which, naturally, I couldn't contradict, disillusioning my new-found friends and storytellers.

I definitely feel that the house had a big influence on my own life. Although not specifically trained for it, I have been in some phase or other of construction work since the mid-thirties. Technical details about our house which have always interested me are the special brick, $1^5/_8$ inches thick by $11^5/_8$ inches long, which Mr. Wright took a special trip to St. Louis to have made. My father and I also believe that this was the first use of welded structural steel in an American house. During the period when father was making preliminary sketches, he knew that a friend of his had been using welded steel girders to build coal loaders for lake and ocean boats. He asked this friend if such girders could be welded suitable for use in a house. The answer was yes, so father passed this on to Mr. Wright. The result: four 15-inch channel beams about 100 to 110 feet long form the backbone of the structure. They were shop fabricated by the Ryerson Steel Co. in Chicago. The rest of the steel was connected by conventional bolting.

132
7. Robie house, daughter's bedroom, courtesy of William Hasbrouck

Robie Jr. (concluding):
Father was very pleased when Mr. Wright telephoned him a month
or so ago from Chicago, talked over old times, gave him the latest
news on our house, and extended an invitation for father to visit
Taliesin West whenever he could. The last time I saw Mr. Wright was
in Chicago in October of 1956 at the Sherman Hotel. He asked about
father, and commented: "A good house for a good man."

3 Footnotes

[1] Sinclair Lewis, *Dodsworth* (New York, 1929), p. 18.
[2] Grant Manson, *Frank Lloyd Wright to 1910: the First Golden Age* (New York, 1958), p. 62.
[3] Frank Lloyd Wright, *An Autobiography* (London, N.D.), p. 117.
[4] *Ibid.,* p. 138.
[5] Manson, *Wright,* p. 188.
[6] Wright, *An Autobiography,* p. 145.
[7] Manson, *Wright,* p. 197.
[8] Wright, *An Autobiography,* p. 114.
[9] *Oak Leaves,* March 29, 1939, p. 85.
[10] *Rochester Times — Union,* April 11, 1955.
[11] *Ibid.*

133
8. Robie house,
under construc-
tion, courtesy of
William
Hasbrouck

4 Howard Van Doren Shaw and the Defense

The reader of the foregoing chapters will naturally raise at least one major question: What sort of person elected to commission conservative domestic architecture in the years 1890–1914? The personality characteristics of the Wright clients are strongly defined. Are the characteristics of the conservative client defined with equal clarity? To answer such questions it is obviously desirable to study the clientele of an architect antithetical to Wright. At first glance the patrons of D. H. Burnham would seem to be highly acceptable, since he is usually thought of as the leader of a kind of counterrevolution. Burnham, however, was mostly concerned with the problem of the tall office building and the railroad terminal, and after 1900, gave a large part of his attention to city planning. The Wrightian revolution was, after all, accomplished in the area of domestic architecture, and it is with houses that we should be concerned. For anyone familiar with the Chicago architectural scene during these years, the name of Howard Van Doren Shaw would automatically suggest itself.

In his own time, Shaw enjoyed a practice built on the solid favor of Chicago's establishment, which, by 1900, already resided largely on the North Shore. He was, in the words of his friend and biographer Thomas Tallmadge, ". . . probably the most highly regarded architect in the sphere of domestic, ecclesiastical, and non commercial architecture in the Middle

1. Howard Van Doren Shaw, c. 1897, courtesy of Mrs. Sylvia Shaw Judson Haskins

138

West."[1] Among his most admired works were the Fourth Presbyterian Church on Michigan Avenue, the Quadrangle Club at the University of Chicago, the Donnelley Printing Building, and the McKinlock Court at the Art Institute. The staple of his practice was, however, an enormous number of large country houses, located both in the city and the North Shore suburbs. These were done for the city's commercial and industrial aristocracy: the Ryersons, Swifts, Donnelleys, and a host of others. It is, we think, fair to call him an "establishment architect."[2]

Born in 1869 (just two years after Wright), Shaw was the son of a prosperous Chicago drygoods merchant of Scotch Presbyterian and Quaker ancestry. Shaw's father was a contemporary of John V. Farwell and active in business before the period when Marshall Field came to dominate retail merchandising in the city. His mother, the former Sarah Van Doren of Brooklyn, came of that famous Dutch stock which has contributed so much to American life. She painted and sketched pleasantly, and it was evidently through her side of the family that artistic talent came to Shaw. Her father was a Princeton graduate and Presbyterian clergyman who played the flute, knew Hebrew and Greek, and could recite long passages from Milton's *Paradise Lost*. One gathers that there was a tradition of polite learning in the family. After graduating from the Har-

3. Shaw house, dining-room table and chairs designed by Shaw, courtesy of Kenneth Krone

139

vard School in Chicago, young Shaw went east to Yale, matriculating with the class of 1890, and then for his architectural training, to the Massachusetts Institute of Technology, which he attended in 1891–1892, combining the work of two years in one. After this professional education he traveled extensively in Europe, making measured drawings and sketches in England, Italy, and Spain.[3]

A word should be said about the social implications of this background for architectural practice in the Chicago of 1890–1914. At that point in history an "Ivy League education" was an even more unusual privilege than it is today. Only a tiny minority of Midwesterners went east to school, and when they returned to their native cities, they constituted a true social elite. Shaw belonged to this group. His education meant that he could talk easily with men like George Vincent, a Yale contemporary who became dean of the arts faculty at the University of Chicago, or John P. Wilson, a distinguished attorney who was a graduate of Williams and the Harvard Law School. On the other hand, his background and assured social and economic position in no way unfitted him for successful personal interaction with self-made men such as the steel tycoon Clayton Mark. From all accounts Shaw was a man of great personal charm. Many of his clients and their sons and daughters have mentioned this quality, and it certainly must have been important for the establishment and maintenance of his practice. Wright, too, possessed the mysterious quality of charm to a remarkable degree, but quite evidently, he was at his best with an entirely different group of people.

After his return to Chicago Shaw entered the office of Jenney and Mundie, where he had also worked on vacation from college. William LeBaron Jenney was, of course, the designer of America's first skyscraper, the famous Home Insurance Building (1884), but none of his superb structural expressionism ever rubbed off on Howard Van Doren Shaw. From the very beginning the young man seems to have reacted negatively to the severe discipline of the Second Leiter Building (1889) and the Ludington (1891); he certainly never followed Jenney in his own business buildings such as the Henneberry Press (1907) and the National Cash Register Company (1914). After a year or so with Jenney, he set up practice for himself in the attic of his father's house on Calumet Avenue, and in 1895 moved to an office downtown. His wife recalled that from that time onward she never knew him to have an idle moment.

Shaw's practice was essentially a one-man affair. His wife wrote that "he wished to do every detail himself." [4] and added that this trait was at least partly responsible for his chronic ill health. His office staff never numbered more than fifteen or twenty, and its outstanding member was unquestionably Da-

vid Adler, who inherited most of his practice. In one respect
Shaw belies our customary picture of the Establishment architect, who is not usually thought of as especially skillful at the
actual business of building. Charles Follen McKim and Stan-
ford White, for example, were not known for their facility with
the carpenter's hammer or the mason's trowel. Shaw, by way
of contrast, was impatient with anyone who did not do as well
as he himself, and he did everything in the building line exceptionally well. His family watched him do carpentry, brick-
laying, cement work, tree-planting, stone-laying, sign-painting,
and shingling. On one occasion he and his gardener built a
sleeping porch at Ragdale, his home in Lake Forest. When
they came to the roof, he sent for a roofer, and the union ques-
tioned the job. Three men stood in his driveway watching him
stain rafters and posts. He never looked up, and they sent a
tin man that afternoon. Needless to say, Shaw was an exact-
ing supervisor for the buildings which he designed, and since
his budgets were hardly ever tight, they are almost always
beautifully put together. This quality of fine workmanship is,
incidentally, one reason that his houses have retained a considerable popularity and a surprising resale value.

Unquestionably this close attention to detail was a cause
of the nervous stomach which bothered Shaw all his adult life.
Examinations at school, public speaking, or a business crisis

brought on an intestinal reaction which, however, vanished as quickly as it came. These reactions never interfered with his work, he never took a vacation unless urged by his doctor, and once away, he usually became well and vigorous. His difficulty did sometimes create embarrassment for his wife, who would decline invitations on the grounds of Shaw's ill health only to encounter a disappointed hostess who had seen her husband bright and early supervising a building on the morning following a party. It is only fair to add that once Shaw bestirred himself to attend a social gathering, he was gay, witty, and delighted that he had been made to go. In short, Shaw's ailment only rarely interfered with either his personal or his professional life. He did not, like Wright, have the constitution of an ox, but until his last illness (pernicious anemia) he was an active and enterprising man.

Shaw's club memberships and civic undertakings are likewise an indication of an energetic disposition. Besides the Yale, University, and City Clubs, he was a founding member of the Cliff Dwellers and also belonged to the Arts Club, both of which were and are important in the artistic life of Chicago. While he also had memberships in the Onwentsia and Shore Acres Country Clubs, he was usually too busy making improvements to Ragdale to spend much time playing golf or tennis at those pleasant institutions. He did, on the other hand, enjoy the social activities which centered there. As befitted a man of his strong religious background, he was for many years treasurer of the Second Presbyterian Church. He was also a trustee of the United Charities of Chicago and a trustee of Illinois College. Clearly Shaw was an active worker for civic improvement. His heart, however, belonged to the Art Institute of Chicago. For many years he was a trustee there and always exceedingly active in its affairs. He was one of the founders of the Burnham Library, and in his will bequeathed to it his own excellent collection of architectural books. He also left to the Institute a small number of architectural materials, including a fine English Gothic doorway. In addition to the McKinlock Court, he designed the Goodman Memorial Theater in the Institute (one of his last works), and at one time gave serious consideration to the idea of becoming its director.

Here again the pattern of his career is at radical variance with that of Wright. To the end of his days Wright was a member of only two clubs, the Players in New York and the Tavern in Chicago. While he was unquestionably an extremely sociable individual, his untrammeled individualism made him a very poor "joiner." In religion he was, of course, an extreme Protestant. In actuality, his religious attitudes were Emersonian, and his entire life might be taken as an illustration of the famous maxim "Whoso would be a man must be a nonconformist."

He was notably averse to working within organizations, and the list of his committee memberships or trusteeships would be short indeed. Although Wright counted numerous reformers and humanitarians among his personal friends, the only "good cause" for which his support is recorded is Margaret Anderson's *Little Review,* a periodical published in Chicago from March 1914 to December 1916. While he enjoyed lecturing and delighted in exhibits of his work at the Chicago Art Institute, the Museum of Modern Art in New York, and elsewhere, his attitude toward museums in general was one of extreme skepticism. Art, he seems to have felt, was too important to be entombed within their marble halls; their emphasis on the art of the past might endanger a true appreciation of the work of the present. Not until the end of his life was he commissioned to do a museum, and then, in the famous Guggenheim, he produced a work which was, at least in part, a protest against the whole tradition of modern painting.[5]

For Howard Van Doren Shaw professional recognition came at an early age. In 1907, at thirty-eight, he was elected Fellow of the American Institute of Architects. Wright never became a Fellow, though he received the Gold Medal of the AIA in 1949 at the age of eighty-two. Aside from such official commissions such as the McKinlock Court and the Goodman Theater, which may have resulted from his personal connection with the Art

Institute, we should note that Shaw was appointed by the United States Battle Monument Commission to do a memorial chapel at Flanders Field and a naval war monument at Brest. This award came at the end of his life so that he did not live to complete the designs. To this day such commissions are the jealously guarded preserve of a small number of architects who have excellent relations with the AIA and the federal government. Finally, he received the Gold Medal of the AIA, its highest award, in 1926, the year of his death. His widow accepted it for him at the 1927 convention.

A word should be said about Shaw's family life because it, too, was in dramatic contrast to that of Wright, and that contrast had implications for his architectural practice. Shaw was married on April 20, 1893, to Frances Wells of Chicago, and like Winston Churchill and his "Clemmie," they lived happily ever after. She came from the same social and economic class as he did, attended Farmington while he was at Yale, and was in every respect equipped to be a perfect helpmeet. In due course she presented him with three attractive daughters, to whom he was truly devoted. Today these ladies recall their father with unfeigned affection. Unlike Wright, Shaw apparently enjoyed his children, and liked to have them around even when he was working. These details are mentioned largely because they are in such complete contradistinction to the story of Frank Lloyd Wright. Whereas Shaw's marriage was an idyll of monogamy, Wright's union with Catherine Tobin foundered on the rocks of temperamental incompatibility and the famous affair with Mrs. Cheney. While Wright's domestic difficulties may not have done his practice so much harm as historians at first believed, there is no doubt whatever of the unfortunate long-term effect. Shaw's stable marriage was, in contrast, a distinct professional asset.

Shaw's architectural style is hard to characterize because he drew on so many sources. Thomas Tallmadge remarked that he disliked French classicism and must have fought many battles against it. Likewise, said Tallmadge, he detested the Italian villa, the Adam interior, and the Norman cottage. In his early years he went through a William Morris or Arts and Crafts phase. This is particularly evident in his own house, Ragdale, built as a summer place at Lake Forest in 1896. It still possesses a few William Morris fabrics. In his maturity the architect whom Shaw most resembled was probably Sir Edwin Lutyens. He liked the soundness and livability of the English domestic tradition as interpreted by Lutyens, and he was happiest when he was working with clients who wanted an American adaptation of an English country house. At the same time he was quite willing to do something Italianate for E. L. Ryerson, Sr., and he drew heavily on Austrian precedent for the village square at Lake Forest. This development, which was financed by the Lake Forest Improvement Trust (one of the most gilt-edged of Chicago investments), has a strong resemblance to an Austrian village marketplace. Among American architects he greatly admired Charles Platt, and he undoubtedly used the Freer Gallery in Washington as a precedent for the McKinlock Court. In short, Shaw was the very model of the cultivated eclectic. His object was always to give the client what he wanted in terms of the most suitable historical precedent. He knew the historic styles perfectly, and his achievement, within the context of eclecticism, is not to be underrated. The Disciples of Christ Church at the University of Chicago will match anything by Ralph Adams Cram, and a number of his houses are of comparable quality.

Since Shaw's career was almost as much identified with Lake Forest as Wright's was with Oak Park, a comparison of these two interesting communities is in order. Christopher Tunnard calls Lake Forest "That most exclusive and romantic of suburbs,"[6] and even today it is an excellent example of the picturesque planning of the mid-nineteenth century. Individual houses are imposing, and the lots often take up several acres, streets are winding, and the visitor will find it difficult to get his bearings. Oak Park, on the other hand, is laid out on a conventional grid; except for the startling number of houses by Wright and his prairie school contemporaries, there is very little to distinguish it from any other prosperous American middle-class suburb. In contrast, Lake Forest, from its earliest days, seems to have had an aristocratic quality. While it was founded prior to the Civil War, its most important period of growth occurred during the late nineteenth and early twentieth centuries when Chicago's commercial aristocracy forsook the city and moved to the North Shore. They were headed by men like Ogden Armour, whose estate is today the campus of Lake Forest Academy. The origins of Oak Park were much more bourgeois in character. Within three decades of its foundation in the eighteen forties, land was being sold not in one- or two-acre lots, but in 50-foot, 75-foot, and 100-foot frontages. It developed as a bedroom suburb for the moderately successful business or professional man who wanted to move his family away from the noise, dirt, and confusion of the city, and as we have indicated earlier, life there had a strong missionary flavor. This was generally lacking in Lake Forest, which tended to focus on the pleasures of the country club and the landed estate.

In keeping with his essentially pragmatic approach, Shaw developed an architecture almost devoid of ideological content. Whereas Sullivan and Wright were much concerned with creating an "architecture of democracy," Shaw simply never gave much thought to the architectural implications of the American political system. Like most of his clients, he voted Republican and let the matter go at that. He likewise made no attempt to express the kind of Midwestern regionalism which marked the work of Sullivan and Wright and of Jens Jensen in landscape architecture. His houses might have been set down anywhere in the United States in any pleasant upper-class suburb. Indeed, one of the finest was done in Radnor, Pennsylvania, for James M. Willcox, the farseeing, aristocratic banker, who, some fifteen years later, commissioned Howe and Lescaze to do the famous Philadelphia Savings Fund Society Building.[7] It is perhaps appropriate to add here that while we have identified Shaw with the North Shore Establishment, he also built in Minneapolis, Racine, Akron, and Davenport, Iowa. He was by no means exclusively a Chicago architect.

Another point of difference with Sullivan, Wright, and the earlier Chicago school was Shaw's complete disinterest in creating an architecture which would express the realities of twentieth-century industrial civilization. None of his houses have anything whatever to do with the technological world in which their owners lived; to a considerable extent they are escapes from that world into an earlier era of hand craftsmanship and gracious living. In this respect it is probably significant that Shaw's literary tastes were essentially conservative. In her memoir of him his wife remarked, "We read chiefly fiction or lighter essays, nothing very abstruse. He loved poetry and never went on a business trip without a volume in his suitcase." [8] We gather that the volume was likely to be *The Oxford Book of English Verse,* rather than *Leaves of Grass* or Sandburg's *Chicago Poems.* These predilections are, of course, in diametrical contrast to those of Sullivan and Wright, who read widely, and somewhat indiscriminately, in their attempts to formulate a philosophical basis for their architecture. In sum, Shaw seems to have been essentially a visual person and a craftsman, not an intellectual, and not in any sense a social critic.

Although Howard Van Doren Shaw and Michelozzo Michelozzi are separated by several centuries in time, there is a curious resemblance between their artistic personalities. Both men failed to embrace the principles of the architectural revolutions with which they were confronted. Both had difficulty in formulating a truly personal style, at least in part because of their desires to accommodate the demands of their clients. Although he adopted some of the external characteristics of the Renaissance style, Michelozzo compromised with the principles upon which it was based. He wanted to speak the new language but continually returned to the old linguistic devices. Hence the Renaissance seems to have been for him largely a matter of details rather than a basically new approach to the problem of architectural design. It is suggestive that today, after several generations of research in the architecture of the quattrocento, he remains a basically obscure figure.

Shaw made even less of an attempt to establish a personal style than Michelozzo. His best work was probably that of his early years, which derives from Voysey. While his later houses are often extremely polished, they lack vitality. His eclecticism was, of course, influenced by the revivalism which was an increasingly powerful force in the American architecture of his time. As with Michelozzo, the demands of his patrons were extremely important. In the Medici Palace Michelozzo retained the fortresslike facade because the Medici did not want the citizens of Florence to envy them. Similarly, Shaw designed for clients who desired houses which reflected their own good manners and culture. They were exceedingly secure people.

We may say, then, that Michelozzo and Shaw failed to understand the principles of the architectural revolutions which were going on around them. It was the genius of Brunelleschi and Wright, separated by five hundred years, that they grasped these principles completely. Michelozzo and Shaw based their architecture upon effect rather than principle. They neglected the theoretical concepts of the revolutionaries. It is significant that neither man ever wrote a book about what he was doing. Wright, of course, wrote voluminously. Brunelleschi's treatises have unhappily been lost. With Michelozzo and Shaw we have a pair of architects who were more concerned with expressing the taste and standards of their clients than with the deeper architectural currents of the age.

In terms of solving the client's program, Shaw's houses are exceptional jobs. Generally speaking, his plans were rectangular, and a number of similarities can be noted among them, though their exteriors varied widely in appearance. In all the country places Shaw created an openness and a sense of relationship with the out-of-doors surprising in so conservative an architect. In our interviews several present-day owners said that they chose their Shaw houses in preference to others of the period which were dark and closed-in. This generalization is particularly true for houses built for summer use, such as the Prentiss Coonley dwelling and the first Finley Barrell house. In these structures there are fewer rooms, and the grounds are extensively developed with terraces, pools, formal gardens, and the like. Shaw very often did his own landscape design, and it tended to be in the formal rather than the naturalistic tradition. Needless to say these gardens, like the houses themselves, require a considerable staff for main- tenance.[9]

The interiors of these buildings may be understood as sequences of compartments, cleverly arranged to lead in several possible directions. Sometimes an entryway will lead to a living room which, in turn, gives on to a more open porch, from which there will be an easy entrance to the garden. Another characteristic path is toward a library, which functions as a kind of retreat and is often more used than the formal living room. These sequences are often extremely inviting and are ordinarily handled with a great subtlety, but there is never any of the dramatic flow of space which is such a noteworthy feature of Wright's designs. On the contrary, they resemble closely the carefully organized series of compartments in the English country houses which Shaw knew and loved so well. Each individual compartment (or "box," to use the Wrightian term) is beautifully scaled and gains additional impact from the fine woodwork, ceramics, and plaster which the financial resources of his patrons made available. The total effect is therefore orderly and harmonious.

On the exterior the facade of the typical Shaw house is a well-proportioned masonry wall, quite traditional in feeling. The material is brick, ordinarily a standard brick rather than the Roman variety favored by Wright. Sometimes, as in the Norton House at Bloomfield Hills, Michigan, Shaw would use a local stone, but his favorite wall material was unquestionably brick, and his detailing was extremely skillful. The entrance is likely to be marked out by a pair of columns or an archway, and in any event, there will be no ambiguity about it. Fenestration was likewise entirely traditional; Shaw was as attached to the double-hung window as Wright was to the casement, and he made no effort to arrange his windows in strips in order to dematerialize the mass. Indeed his effort was in just the opposite direction. Similarly his houses usually have strong corners, whereas Wright often tended to dissolve his corners in sheets of glass. Leaded glass, which was much favored by Wright and the other prairie architects, was rarely, if ever, used by Shaw. At the rear he liked tall French windows opening out onto terraces and gardens.

As one studies these houses, he will inevitably feel that they are well proportioned, dignified structures, perfectly suited to the requirements of their exceedingly conservative owners. Looked at objectively, they have considerable architectural distinction, although none, needless to say, is in a class with the great creations of Wright. All, however, are excellent solutions to the programs presented by the clients. That is, they are proper settings for the kind of family life and social gatherings which took place within their walls. In quality they may quite reasonably be compared with the town houses of McKim, Mead, and White in New York City. Here, too, we have elegant, if eclectic, solutions for an extremely conservative clientele. Indeed, it is interesting to note that Herbert Croly, who was Shaw's most sympathetic contemporary critic, was also enthusiastic about the work of the New York firm. His appreciation of Shaw deserves at least a word of comment.

Croly, who is today known as an ideologue of the Progressive Movement rather than as an architectural critic, was associate editor of the *Architectural Record* from 1901 to 1907 and thereafter a contributing editor for many years. Unlike his older colleague Montgomery Schuyler, Croly took a critical position grounded on sociological considerations rather than an understanding of architectural design. Granting that the eclecticism of the Gilded Age had led to a blurring of coherent form and plan, Croly nonetheless condoned the movement as the proper expression of an economically vigorous and socially fluid nation. In 1903, however, American architecture stood in need of tradition and discipline. In that year he wrote, "There can be no doubt that the increasing authority of certain special types of design constitutes the line of progress for American architecture. The architect more than any other artist is dependent upon precedent. The material of his work is not derived from life but from the work of his predecessors. His individual genius counts for less than in other arts; the general social and particular technical standard count for more." [10] It is not surprising that Croly spoke well of McKim, Mead, and White nor that he hailed Shaw in 1907 with a lengthy article illustrating the Bartlett, first Ryerson, Swift, and Baker houses; these buildings, said Croly, placed Shaw among the architects in the country whose houses were likely to be a pleasure to the owner, an example to other architects, and a consolation to the critic. Six years later, in 1913, Croly and C. M. Price of the *Record* wrote an even more laudatory treatment of Shaw for that journal. During the next decade Shaw's work was also published in *The Western Architect* and *The Brickbuilder* and in such decidedly upper-class periodicals as *The Spur* and *Country Life in America*. Obviously he never lacked for publicity. It is especially significant that Croly, whose connections with the Eastern Establishment were intimate, thought so well of him.

How did Frank Lloyd Wright see his contemporary? In his *A Testament* (published in 1957) he recalled Shaw as a member of a luncheon club of young architects during the nineties. The group included Hugh Garden, Richard Schmidt, Dwight Perkins, and various other men later to achieve fame. He added that he felt Shaw was always sympathetic to his work but was never able to break away from the English colonial. More important is a section from Wright's famous 1918 address on *Chicago Culture*:

One of Chicago's influential admirable architects, and one who has built some good houses and fine industrial buildings, told me not long ago of a wealthy widow from some town down in the Middle West who came to ask him to build a monument to her husband, a local politician some months dead. She wanted to buy an exact replica of the Greek monument to Lysicrates, to be set up on their lot in the home town cemetery. To her, a beautiful thought for her dead husband.

Hoping to dissuade her, Mr. Shaw told her of the great cost of such an undertaking. But happening to go East about that time, he met some of the influential architects of New York, Boston, and Philadelphia. At dinner he told the story and to his surprise they said, "By all means go back and build it for her; a beautiful thing like that couldn't fail to be educational." There it is. The costly fallacy behind all this stark, staring, naked. The shameless irrelevant use of a beautiful thing its abuse, therefore, justified as educational! With such advocates on top, what chance has the eternal fitness of things underneath?

Abuse, you see, is "academic" now.

Another traveled rich woman adored the Petit Trianon. She must have it for a house, only it was a story too low. So Mr. Shaw put another story on the Trianon for her. If he had not done it someone else would have and would probably have done it worse. Mr. Shaw said so.

I sneered and he turned and showed me a Gothic building he had just finished as a home for some Chicago businessman and asked if

I liked it any better. It was chaste, severe, very well done like a little stage setting of a twelfth century play, of course, with modern improvements. I utterly failed to imagine entering it other than in costume. And yet this hard-headed Chicago businessman elected to buy Gothic. That was his cultural expedient. Really, are we too, in Chicago, plundering the old world of all its finery and dressing ourselves up in it regardless as a kind of masquerade? I can see it as great fun (very expensive fun), but how can it be seen as culture when the essence of all true culture is a *development* of self-expression.[11]

These words, written at a time when the triumph of eclecticism appeared secure, show Wright's mingled contempt and envy for his rival. Shaw had done some good houses and fine industrial buildings, yet he was willing to compromise by doing buildings in period dress. In Wright's terms Shaw's problem was not one of ability—that quality he possessed in large measure—but of character. The passage is also, of course, a reflection of Wright's profound disgust with the direction which culture was taking in Chicago. He was simply outraged by the city's subservience to Eastern taste.

On Shaw's part, he thought of Wright as a friend, admired his work, and liked him personally, though he had no inclination whatever to follow his professional leadership. His daughter recalls that the two men enjoyed each other enormously on a trip to the Orient in 1917 when Shaw was on vacation and Wright was en route to Japan to work on the Imperial Hotel in

Tokyo. A few years later, in 1923, Wright sent Shaw photographs of the finished building and asked his advice on a possible reply to an attack on the work by the California architect Louis Mullgardt. After saying how much he and his office staff had enjoyed the pictures, Shaw wrote that the best course would be to ignore the slur. "Your work," he remarked, "is bound to live; I cannot say the same of his, and certainly nothing else will keep his name alive. What is the use of spreading a manifestly personal and commercial attack? The best thing is to let it die where it is." [12] It is interesting that in Wright's subsequent publications on the Imperial Hotel he made no mention of the article by Mullgardt. It has, in fact, dropped from sight altogether as Shaw suggested it would.

In many respects the relationship of Wright and Shaw was paradoxical. Wright can be thought of as the embattled general of an army besieging a fortified city. Shaw may be seen as the commander of the defending troops, who, however, was never really conscious that he was leading a defense. It is, of course, indicative of Shaw's complete security in his position that he never bothered to write any explanation of what he was doing. Wright, of course, was continually indulging in polemics, and lived to see the ultimate triumph of his cause insofar as modern architecture was widely accepted by the North Shore Establishment.

Shaw's clients may be conveniently divided into a series of circles. In the first group there were the sons of the men who had arrived in Chicago before the Civil War and made large fortunes during the General Grant era. Thus Shaw never built anything for the original Gustavus Swift, who founded the meat-packing firm, but he did large houses for his sons Gustavus, Jr., and Louis, as well as for Edward Morris, who inherited the control of the rival firm of Morris and Company. Similarly, he never built a house for R. R. Donnelley, who founded the printing firm, but he did country places for his sons Reuben and Thomas and several buildings for the company as well. Among the older generation of merchant princes his only important client was Adolphus Clay Bartlett, the wholesale hardware magnate, for whom he built a handsome country house at Lake Geneva, Wisconsin, in 1907. His son, Frederick Bartlett, was an amateur painter and good friend of Shaw's; he is important in the cultural history of Chicago for the magnificent collection of French paintings which he gave to the Art Institute in memory of his wife.

This second generation of the merchant aristocracy were generally able, hard-driving men who went into the family business and expanded it enormously. Edward L. Ryerson is a good example. Under his leadership Ryerson Steel grew to be the largest independent steel producer in the country (in 1935

the company became a wholly owned subsidiary of Inland
Steel Corporation). Sometimes these men were college-edu-
cated, sometimes they were not. Ryerson was class of '76 at
Yale (Sheffield), but the only education of Swift and Morris
was in the public schools of Chicago. In general their orientation was to success in business and to leisure-time fulfillment
through golf, sailing, riding, and perhaps fishing or hunting.
An important minority took an active interest in the Art Institute. For the most part, however, they were intensely competitive, viewing business as a kind of war. Arthur Meeker, who
knew them well, depicted them beautifully in a passage in his
semi-autobiographical novel *Prairie Avenue*:

. . . all these young men were exactly alike: round headed and burly,
strident of voice and aggressively cheery. They were hard-working,
hard-playing, hard-thinking, hard-drinking, as their fathers had been
before them. Many, perhaps, had to work even harder. In a society
that failed to recognize the law of primogeniture the great pioneer
fortunes were split into sections as their founders disappeared.[13]

This society scoffed at the idea of a leisure class.

Closely related to these scions of the old aristocracy was a
group of new men, equally capable and ambitious. These people fought their way to the top of the economic pyramid by
sheer ability without the benefit of established financial position. Ordinarily, they came from outside Chicago and were not
so well educated as the sons of the old aristocracy. Some-

times, indeed, they were graduates of the school of hard knocks. William V. Kelley and Donald R. McLennan may be taken as representatives of the new arrivals. Kelley, a native of Gratis, Ohio, attended business college in Springfield, Ohio, and came to Chicago to make a fortune in the steel industry. McLennan, who was born in Duluth, went to business school there, and in Chicago founded the insurance firm which ultimately became Marsh and McLennan. Another member of this group was Robert P. Lamont, who was born in Detroit, educated at the University of Michigan, and finally became Secretary of Commerce under President Hoover.

It may be noted here that the clients of Frank Lloyd Wright were also self-made men but that they differed from Shaw's patrons in certain important ways. The Shaw clients were generally much more successful economically, and were therefore thrown into closer contact with the city's first aristocracy, which controlled its largest enterprises. Kelley and Lamont, for example, were both in the steel business, and would almost inevitably have had a good deal of contact with Ryerson. Such contact was much less likely for men like Winslow and W. E. Martin. This social interaction with the old aristocracy meant that they tended to share its cultural tastes and leisure-time recreations. By using the Ryersons, Swifts, and Donnelleys as models, they escaped the tension which usually accompanies extreme social mobility. They were therefore less likely than the Wright clients to strike out on their own. In addition, they displayed none of the internalized psychology which is so characteristic of the Wright clients. None was musical, and none was an inventor. They tended to be forceful, gregarious salesmen and executives who accepted the traditional channels for the release of those energies which did not go into their business hours. It is not surprising that for their houses they went to Shaw rather than to Wright.

A third, and somewhat surprising, circle of Shaw clients was centered in the University of Chicago. These were undoubtedly headed by Professor George Vincent of the sociology department, who later became dean of the faculties at Chicago, then president of the University of Minnesota, and finally president of the Rockefeller Foundation. Like Shaw, Vincent was a Yale man, and it is likely that their paths crossed while the two men were at New Haven. Vincent's career, which was certainly distinguished, indicates that he possessed a persuasive personality, and he is probably responsible for the awarding of certain other commissions in the university area, notably the house for Mrs. William Rainey Harper, built after her husband's death, and perhaps the Quadrangle Club of 1920. Another important member of this academic circle was Edgar J. Goodspeed, the famous Orientalist, widely known for his translation of the Bible. Shaw built him a house in 1910.

Closely linked with the university community was an additional group of clients whose interests led them, for one reason or another, to build in the Kenwood area rather than the more fashionable near North Side. Such a person was the publisher Henry Hoyt Hilton, who was the guiding genius of Ginn and Company. The house which Shaw built for him on Woodlawn Avenue later became the official residence of the chancellor of the university. Not too far from this house was the home of Morris Rosenwald, brother of the famous philanthropist, Julius. It was located at 4924 Woodlawn, just eight blocks from the famous Robie House. The location of these early town houses near the university is, in fact, extremely significant. The Kenwood district is an area of substantial upper-middle-class dwellings. It is very definitely not a showcase for the houses of the rich. Woodlawn was hardly a street of palaces, like Prairie Avenue in the eighties and nineties. Wright's Robie and Heller houses, like his McArthur, Blossom, and Harlan dwellings, which are situated nearby, are to be understood as homes for families in the same economic bracket as the Vincents, Goodspeeds, and Hiltons. Except for a few isolated examples like the Edward Morris house on Drexel Boulevard, Shaw's domestic practice did not include any really large commissions until about 1907 or 1908, when he began to do truly imposing country places in the Lake Forest area. Those years were turning points in his practice, as they were with Wright. Prior to that time the clients of the two men might be termed in general quite similar economically. The attraction of these university clients to Shaw is, on the face of it, somewhat mysterious. The place was in a period of great intellectual vigor and should logically have been receptive to new ideas in architecture, as it was in the social and physical sciences. The key to the situation probably lies in the influence of Vincent and the trustees, most of whom came from the business environment of the city.

In the University of Chicago area, then, a significant circle of Shaw clients built dwellings near an almost equally important group of Wright clients. This is a situation which throws light on the problem of access, as does the situation of the Coonley brothers. What led Prentiss Coonley to build his Shaw house in Lake Forest at the same time that his brother was building a house by Wright in Riverside? According to Miss Eleanor Coonley, her father was familiar with Wright's work but chose Shaw as his architect. What was the basis for his choice? The brothers were good friends and visited each other frequently; they must have had some interesting conversations about their houses. While it is impossible to be certain, we would suggest that the key to the problem is to be found in Avery

Coonley's somewhat internalized personality. Quite clearly he was never as happy in the business world as his brother, and he was also less of a joiner. His club memberships, for example, were limited in number and not of major importance to him. Both brothers enjoyed riding, but Prentiss Coonley was Master of the Onwentsia Hunt. Coupled with this internalized and individuated personality was the influence of Queene Ferry Coonley, an avid architectural amateur. Unlike her sister-in-law, who was distinguished for her religious and aesthetic interests, Mrs. Prentiss Coonley seems to have been a conventional person. Her recreation was gardening, not Christian Science.

In similar fashion Shaw's clients in the University of Chicago area were conventional people, lacking the streak of individuality which is so apparent in the Wright patrons. In essential character there is very little which sets apart George Vincent from Shaw's businessman clients; he was simply an empire builder in another sphere. Much the same thing could be said about the publisher Henry Hilton, who was a kind of fringe member of the university community. In view of the fact that the Heller House (1897) and the Robie House (1908–1909) were visible on Woodlawn Avenue when they built, it is hard to believe that men as alert as Vincent and Hilton were unacquainted with Wright's work; he was, after all, sufficiently linked with the university community to spend time and some of his own money on the ill-fated Como Orchards scheme of 1908, a vacation community in Montana for a group of professors. The evidence suggests that the university circle made a deliberate choice on the basis of their total personality structure. Then, too, it is well to point out that universities were not at this time gatherings of socially mobile people, as they tend to be today. The Wright clients were an essentially mobile group, and at this period these personalities were generally to be found outside the academic environment.

Finally, Shaw's clientele included a number of important Midwestern businessmen whose affairs brought them to Chicago more or less frequently. In the city they encountered Shaw or his patrons and returned to their hometowns determined to build a fashionable house. The process was, of course, akin to that by which Wright acquired his Buffalo commissions through W. E. Martin of Oak Park. Warren C. Fairbanks of Indianapolis is a good example of Shaw's provincial clients. Born in 1878 into an Indiana family important in Republican politics (his father was Vice President under Theodore Roosevelt), he graduated from Ohio Wesleyan in 1898, served in the Spanish-American War, and thereafter was active in several small manufacturing concerns as well as managing his father's estate. In 1922 he became publisher of the *Indianapolis News,* a position which he filled with considerable distinction; the paper won several Pulitzer awards under his guidance. In addition he was, at various times, president of the Indiana Switch and Frog Company, and a director of the Pure Oil Company, Metropolitan Gas and Electric, and Union Gas and Electric. Active in civic affairs, he was director of the Indiana Unemployment Relief Commission under President Hoover, and a trustee of Methodist Hospital in Indianapolis. In that city he belonged to the University, Indiana Athletic, Columbia and Woodstock Country Clubs, and in Chicago to the University, Casino, Onwentsia, Racquet, and Saddle and Cycle. His chief diversions were reading, riding, and hunting, and he built his Shaw house in 1912. The portrait of Charles S. Pillsbury of the famous Minneapolis Flour Milling family is similar in general outline, as is that of Arthur Marks, a tycoon of the rubber industry in Akron. They built their houses in 1921 and 1915 respectively. Thus the style of Shaw spread throughout the region, and versions of it can be found in several cities.

When we begin to compare the Shaw clients with those of Wright, the first element of difference which emerges is in education. Whereas only a few of Wright's patrons had college training, a large percentage of Shaw's had bachelor's degrees, most of them from the Ivy League. A surprising number of these were from Yale, and since Shaw himself was a Yale man, one begins to suspect something like a British "old boy net." The education of the three physicians whom we have been able to trace is particularly impressive, and certainly contributed to their leadership in the medical community of Chicago. All had postgraduate training in Germany, which, in the late nineteenth century, led the world in medicine and surgery. Dr. Bertram W. Sippy was professor of medicine at Rush Medical College, Dr. Nathan Smith Davis was dean at Northwestern, and Dr. William Casselberry pioneered in the establishment of the ear, nose, and throat specialty in the city. The lawyers were almost equally distinguished. John P. Wilson, for example, was a partner in a firm which handled the family interests and much of the corporate business of the Armours, Swifts, and McCormicks. Others with law degrees, like Leverett Thompson and Wallace DeWolf, did not practice but were active in the real estate field. In general it is clear that Shaw's clients possessed a higher level of formal education than those of Wright.

Lawyers and doctors were, of course, a minority. The majority were businessmen, about equally divided between manufacturers and processors on the one hand, and dealers in the various kinds of commercial paper on the other. While it is difficult to summarize their activities, we may say that both groups were primarily concerned with the expansion of the market. The career of Edward Ryerson has already been cited; Gustavus Swift, Jr., and Edward Morris were equally effective in the packing industry. These men were quick to see the opportunities and to supply the emerging needs of the economy. Thus Reuben Donnelley compiled Chicago's first telephone directory, and in addition to his duties with the family printing firm, was a member of a brokerage firm, and president of the Chicago Stock Exchange 1901–1903. While all were abundantly endowed with that overwhelming energy which has always characterized the American businessman, except for Arthur H. Marks of Akron none seems to have been very much interested in technology. Marks, a gifted industrial chemist, discovered an alkali-reclaiming method which made possible the salvaging of scrap rubber by enabling large amounts of it to be combined with crude rubber without sacrificing quality. It was a crucial process for the development of the industry; he patented it, and eventually became vice president of Goodrich Rubber and a multimillionaire. As a hobby Marks also became interested in the pipe organ and organ music, and eventually had one or more organ patents assigned to him. More than any of the Shaw clients, he resembled the type of businessman who ordinarily went to Wright for his house.

For their avocations these men socialized with each other, traveled, and played golf. The number of club memberships is truly astonishing, and very often indicates rather higher social status than those of the Wright clients. Many belonged to the Chicago Club, which possessed the wealthiest membership in the city; Marshall Field and George Pullman were among its habitués. Similarly the Onwentsia was probably the favorite country club, with the Old Elm running a close second for those who were "serious golfers." The typical client belonged to two or three downtown clubs, and one or two which reflected his personal interest, such as the Arts or the Chicago Yacht. A fair number went in for such distinctly upper-class sports as sailing and horseback riding. Prentiss Coonley, brother of Avery, was Master of the Onwentsia Hunt, and Stuyvesant Peabody was president of the Illinois Turf Association. In Minneapolis the leisure-time activities of Charles S. Pillsbury reflected the same pattern. He was a member of the Minneapolis Club (downtown), of the Woodhill Country Club, which, in addition to the usual range of activities, sponsors an annual horse show, and of the Keswick (Virginia) Hunt Club. While many of the Wright clients played golf, only one or two sailed or rode to hounds. Among the Shaw clients none was an amateur photographer like Nathan Moore, and none had a basement workshop in the manner of W. H. Winslow and Charles E. Roberts. They were an active, not an introspective, group.

On the cultural side many of these men took subscriptions

to the Chicago Symphony, and a significant minority were active in the affairs of the Art Institute. Some of them were serious collectors. Wallace DeWolf was a painter himself, and also collected the work of Anders Zorn and Seymour Haden. Leverett Thompson had a fine collection of French and English furniture. In Detroit Strong Vincent Norton furnished his house with English antiques, most of which he either gave or loaned to the Norton Art Gallery in West Palm Beach, Florida. Walter S. Brewster was almost as much involved in the Chicago Art Institute as Howard Van Doren Shaw. He was a trustee there as well as of the American Academy in Rome, and frequently traveled in Europe. These interests are particularly significant when compared with the almost complete lack of concern with the Art Institute displayed by Wright's clients. Except for Japanese prints, an interest fostered by Wright himself, none collected any sort of art, and none took any part in the management of the Art Institute. Without the Shaw clients, particularly the Bartlett family, it is hard to see how the place would have achieved its present eminence.

The attitude toward music in the two groups is also strikingly different. While some attended symphony concerts, none exhibited the intense commitment to music which we notice in the Winslow, Heurtley, and Little families. Charles Pillsbury, for example, was a director of the Minneapolis Orchestral Association and a generous contributor to its support, but he himself never played an instrument or sang in a chorus. Much the same thing can be said of his opposite numbers in Chicago and of their wives. Apparently, musical skills and interests were not widely diffused among the patrons of Shaw. Of the wives only Mrs. William Rainey Harper played an instrument (the piano), and she does not seem to have been especially serious about it. Except for the previously mentioned Arthur H. Marks house, we encounter no case of an interior being designed as a kind of miniature concert hall.

For the most part the wives of the Shaw clients do not emerge from this study as strongly marked personalities. Most seem to have been content with household management and a genteel round of social activities. In contrast to the wives of the Wright clients, none was active in the suffrage movement, and their civic concerns seem also to have been more limited. Often they spent a good bit of time at the various country clubs to which their families belonged, and we have the impression that many were skilled golfers and tennis players. Socially these women placed much emphasis on "being in the right place at the right time," as one of them put it; often their daughters made formal debuts, as did Shaw's own children. The society pages of the Chicago papers are a revealing record of their activities.

One area in which these women were exceedingly active was home furnishing. With these couples there was probably a sharper split between the roles of husband and wife in the construction and furnishing of the house than with the Wright clients. The husband tended to work closely with Shaw on what was regarded as the essentially masculine business of building, while the wife took almost complete charge of interior decoration, often working with the architect as mentor. Since Shaw's own taste was conservative and English, many of these women developed into collectors of antique furniture, old china, and so forth. We can obtain a graphic impression of the sort of effect which was sought in a contemporary description of the interior of the house which Shaw built for Gustavus Swift, Jr. "The problems of the decoration of the interior," we are told, "have been harmoniously worked out by the architect, with the help of the owners, with the most satisfactory results." Said the writer for the *Spur*:

One's first impression of the interior is of spaciousness and dignity. The rooms are well balanced and they have wide spaces and long vistas. The furnishings have been so carefully considered in relation to the lines of each room that the effect is one of repose as well as harmony. There are few embellishments or ornaments, and these are all quite in keeping with the character of the house.

Entrance is through a grilled gate into an enclosed vestibule of glass. The stone ceiling is groined and the lighting is from a lantern

of intricate design in wrought iron and pendant from an ornament of
clustered carved stone flowers. Carved stone boxes on either side of
the entrance hold box trees. From the entrance hall, through a door of
rough, unpolished wood opened by iron hasps, one enters the great
hall, which is much like the great hall in an English castle, somewhat
modified for city needs. Here is a huge fireplace of carved stone and
flanking it are two tall flambeaux in which candles burn on festive
occasions. High in the wall an oriel window is set in the wood and
plaster. From this window, opening from the living room on the second floor, one looks down upon the great hall, which has a very beautiful stairway of white oak, with the rails, spindles, and strings all cut
from solid timbers. The color has a decided gray tone which is especially pleasing to the discriminating eye in a room of this kind, on
account of the soft artistic effect.[14]

Gustavus Swift, Jr., was one of those businessmen who was
completely absorbed in the affairs of his company. We know
from our interview that his wife was primarily responsible for
all this magnificence.

Politically these people displayed the same ardent Republicanism as the Wright clients. While many of the men made
donations to the party, only a few, such as Warren Fairbanks
and Moses Wentworth, an attorney who served three terms in
the Illinois State Legislature, were truly influential in party affairs. Quite clearly they were interested in economic rather
than political power. In general they took no part in the exceedingly grimy municipal politics of Chicago and did not respond

to the injunctions of Theodore Roosevelt to involve themselves in the process of government. They were much too occupied with their business affairs to do so. Probably the most liberal was Prentiss Coonley, who actually went to Washington during the New Deal period. On the other hand, many of these men were willing to spend substantial amounts of time running nonpolitical civic institutions. Leverett Thompson spent twenty years on the board of the Chicago Y.M.C.A., both Clayton Mark and A. C. Bartlett served on the Board of Education, and many others were trustees of various Chicago hospitals. Benjamin E. Bensinger and Louis B. Kuppenheimer were active in Jewish charitable work, and Morris Rosenwald was president of the Home for Jewish Friendless and Working Girls. In short, politics, as normally considered, was not an area of activity for the Shaw clients, but they were by no means unwilling to accept nonpolitical civic responsibilities.

For most of them religion was as conventional an affair as Republican political affiliation. Almost all were church members, but few were active as vestrymen, trustees, or in other positions of responsibility. The brewer Thomas Fortune, who was an Irish immigrant, and the Philadelphia banker James Willcox were the only Roman Catholics we have been able to find. It is probable that the Jewish clients—the Bensingers, Schaffners, Beckers, and Rosenwalds—were somewhat more concerned with religion than the Protestants, but this concern usually took the form of work for Jewish charitable organizations. Among the Shaw clients only William Pelouze, a manufacturer who built a country house at Lake Geneva in 1920, was a Unitarian. In religion, as in so many other aspects of life, they were thoroughly conventional.

The manner in which Shaw acquired this clientele is easy to perceive. His patrons participated in interlocking networks of club memberships, corporate boards, institutional trustee-ships, and alumni associations. Shaw himself participated in a number of these and after his first successes in the nineties, he soon came to be known in Chicago upper-class circles as a soundly conservative designer who built solidly constructed, extremely livable houses. He would do nothing "radical" or "out of the way." Wright was not known in these circles, or if he was, was viewed in an unfavorable light. One surviving Shaw client remarked that Wright's houses looked like gas stations. Shaw's enormous popularity in the Lake Forest area was undoubtedly fostered by his own shrewd (but not calculated) construction of a summer place in that community in 1896. His residence there meant that he was available in the area at the outset of a tremendous building boom. It suggested that he could easily supervise the houses which were going up in close proximity to his own. At the same time his continued winter residence in the city and his maintenance of an office there allowed him to keep up his contacts in the business world, which offered him a number of important nondomestic commissions. It was an ideal arrangement.

If, then, we follow Max Weber and try to imagine an ideal Shaw client, we may picture him as a businessman born into sufficiently favorable circumstances so that his parents can give him some degree of higher education. Indeed, there is a strong probability that he will have a degree from an Ivy League school. In his business he will ordinarily be concerned with manufacturing, processing, or commercial paper. Whether his line of work is "hard" or "soft," he will be primarily concerned with the expansion of the market and the creation of wants. In contradistinction to the Wright clients, he will not customarily be much concerned with the technological side of his work. He is intensely competitive, and his efforts usually bring him a very substantial measure of success, so that when he builds a house, money is not a major problem. Besides serving as an officer of his own firm, he is likely to be a director of two or three others. In religion he is Protestant, in politics, Republican. He may contribute financially to the support of the church and the party, but will not otherwise be active.

His leisure-time pursuits reveal him to be a thoroughly ex-

ternalized personality who revels in the company of his fellows.
He belongs to at least five or six clubs, two or three in the city,
and the others devoted to golf, tennis, sailing, or horseback
riding. These clubs constitute a major channel for the employment of his psychic energy. His wife will come from the same
social and economic background as he himself, and she will
share his interest in outdoor diversions. She may have gone to
finishing school while he was attending Harvard or Yale. They
will have a small family, ordinarily two or three children. In the
house-building project he will take the lead in working with the
architect, while she will be in charge of furnishing the interior.
Neither husband nor wife will be at all interested in acquiring
contemporary furniture or the more advanced varieties of
modern painting. On the contrary, their taste is conservative
and English in its orientation. If it is a country place, both may
share an interest in landscape gardening.

Because the family is quite sociable, the program of the
house is likely to stress spaces for entertaining and guest
rooms in addition to the standard requirements of bedrooms,
baths, kitchens, and so forth. A spacious entryway is highly
desirable, and servants' quarters may be provided. The living
room should be suitable for cocktail parties and receptions; a
piano will, however, not ordinarily be part of its equipment. The

dining room should be able to accommodate formal dinner parties without any trouble. In short, the house should be a proper setting for the upper-class life of its owners. It is a symbol of achieved status and a badge of membership in the North Shore Establishment.

If we compare the Shaw clients with the Wright clients as a group, we perceive that they are in general better educated, more successful economically, more sociable, and more conventional in their leisure-time activities. The degree of economic achievement is, in fact, so great that they seem to represent a remarkable portion of the business elite of Chicago. The provincial clients such as Pillsbury and Fairbanks were also among the business leaders in their cities. Shaw must have built a good many houses which were unbudgeted. Their major energies were turned to business success, active recreation, and civic affairs. They are externalized personalities, rarely given to reflection, introspection, or the individualized kind of hobby represented by the basement workshop. In all these respects they differ from the Wright clients. From this analysis we conclude that the patrons for the Wrightian innovations lie in a stratum of the American middle class which had little to do with the North Shore Establishment. If Wright had, by chance, located his studio in Lake Forest, he might very well

have had to move to Oak Park. It was part of his genius that he
made the right move in the first place.

4 Footnotes

[1] Article on Howard Van Doren Shaw by Thomas Tallmadge in the *Dictionary of American Biography.*

[2] We use the term "Establishment" to refer to that group of people who controlled the official cultural life of Chicago. They sat on the Board of Directors of the Art Institute, were active in the affairs of the Symphony, were trustees of the University, and so on. Ordinarily, they belonged to the same clubs, went to the same churches, and were very often acquainted socially.

[3] For this information we have relied on a memoir by Frances Wells Shaw, *Concerning Howard Van Doren Shaw.* It was evidently written shortly after his death in 1926 and may be found in the Burnham Library of the Chicago Art Institute.

[4] *Ibid.*

[5] Writings by and about Frank Lloyd Wright are voluminous. The attitudes recorded herein are scattered through a number of books. Authority for the contribution to the *Little Review* is Bernard Duffey, *The Chicago Renaissance* (East Lansing, 1956), p. 190.

[6] Christopher Tunnard, *The City of Man* (New York, 1953), p. 206.

[7] For material on Willcox, see William Jordy, "PSFS: Its Development and Significance in Modern Architecture," *Journal of the Society of Architectural Historians*, XXI (1962), pp. 47–83.

[8] Frances Wells Shaw, *Concerning Shaw,* p. 5.

[9] Shaw's landscape design is well illustrated in the articles by Herbert Croly, "Some Recent Work of Mr. Howard Shaw," *Architectural Record*, XXII (1907), pp. 422–453, and "The Recent Work of Howard Shaw," *Architectural Record,* XXXII (1913), pp. 285–329.

182

[10] Herbert Croly, *Houses for Town and Country* (New York, 1903), p. 30.
[11] Frank Lloyd Wright, "Chicago Culture," in *Frank Lloyd Wright on Architecture,* ed. Frederick Gutheim (New York, 1941), pp. 86–87.
[12] Howard Van Doren Shaw to Frank Lloyd Wright, January 11, 1923. Letter in possession of Chicago Architectural Photographing Co.
[13] Arthur Meeker, *Prairie Avenue* (New York, 1949), p. 284.
[14] Amy L. Paulding, "The Home of Gustavus Swift, Jr.," *The Spur,* April 1, 1919, pp. 45–47.

5 Profiles of Shaw Clients

Pp. 197–203

1. Clayton Mark,
courtesy of Mark
Manufacturing
Corporation

As with the Wright clients, we offer here a series of character sketches of representative Shaw clients. They are chosen to illustrate the milieu in which the architect moved and the type of person who characteristically went to him for a house. The reader is invited to compare the approaches to religion, politics, occupation, family life, and leisure-time activity of these individuals with those of the Wright clients. We are conscious that there is less information on the actual building projects than with the first group. The reason is undoubtedly that the houses were conventional in construction, liberally budgeted, and on the whole went smoothly.

Mr. and Mrs. Reuben Hamilton Donnelley (Lake Forest, 1907)

Reuben H. Donnelley was born in Brantford, Ontario, in 1864 and brought to Chicago at the age of two months. He can therefore be classed as a native Chicagoan, and indeed, he was identified with the city throughout his entire career. Many of Shaw's clients had interests which took them to Washington, D.C., or to various other parts of the country at different times in their lives, but Donnelley was a Chicagoan all his life. He was educated in the public schools and attended the University of Chicago through his junior year, leaving in 1884 to enter the family firm of R. R. Donnelley and Sons. This enterprise had been founded by his father, an energetic Canadian

2. Mark house, front elevation, *Architectural Record*, vol. XLII, No. 6, December 1917

printer, whose venture grew as the city's economy expanded, until it became one of the country's largest printing houses, which it remains today. The Lakeside Press is still widely known for the quality of its work.

His first job with the firm was the compilation and publication of the city directory; he subsequently became secretary and treasurer and then vice president. In 1886 he began to publish in his own name the classified telephone directory for Chicago, and this business was finally incorporated as the Reuben H. Donnelley Corporation in 1917, of which he was president. This firm also published telephone directories in New York, Boston, New Haven, St. Louis, and Los Angeles. His business career was not, however, a string of unbroken successes. In 1898 he formed, with Newell C. Knight, the brokerage firm of Knight, Donnelley & Company, member of the New York and Chicago Stock Exchanges and the Chicago Board of Trade. It failed in 1905, and thereafter Donnelley devoted all his energy to the publishing business. In this field he amassed a substantial fortune, and in 1928, while ill in a hospital, announced that he had entirely liquidated the indebtedness of $650,000, with interest, left by the failure twenty-one years previously, but from which the courts had absolved him of all personal responsibility.

In his personal life Donnelley was one of those men with a

3. Mark house,
entrance, *Archi-
tectural Record,*
vol. XLII, No. 6,
December 1917
187

genius for friendship. Among his close acquaintances were
the banker and broker James O. Hinkley, the steel magnate
William V. Kelley, and the attorney and art collector Wallace
DeWolf (all of them Shaw clients). An extremely sociable individual he was a member of the Arts, Casino, Union League,
and Chicago Clubs in the city, and of the Onwentsia, Old Elm,
and Shore Acres Country Clubs on the North Shore. In addition he was a life member of the Art Institute and the Field
Museum and belonged to the Chicago Advertising Club, the
Horticultural Society, and the Grand Island Shooting Club. To
an astonishing degree his tastes were those of an English
country gentleman—hunting, boating, and the outdoor life. He
loved blooded dogs, and was an expert with the gun, often
breaking one hundred clay pigeons in succession. Fond of art,
he collected etchings and paintings. His favorite books were
biographies, the novels of Dickens, and as a boy, James Feni-
more Cooper, Horatio Alger, and Oliver Optic. He was, one
feels, exactly the sort of person who should have lived in a
Shaw house.

Shaw's connection with the Donnelley family was a close
one. In 1911 he built the Lakeside Press Building for the company, and he also did a house in Lake Forest for Thomas E.
Donnelley, who was its president. In the same fashion a few
years later he designed an office building in New York City for

4. Mark house, side elevation, *Architectural Record,* vol. XLII, No. 6, December 1917

188

the Goodrich Rubber Company and shortly thereafter did houses outside Akron for B. G. Work, its president, and Arthur Marks, its engineering genius. Success with a domestic commission led to a business building, and the contrary could also be true.

Henry Hoyt Hilton (Chicago, Illinois, 1911)

The publisher Henry H. Hilton was born in Cambridge, Massachusetts, in 1868 of old New England stock. After preparation in the public schools of Lowell, he went on to Dartmouth College, where he received an A.B. degree in 1890. That October he became an agent in rural New England for Ginn and Company, and from the start went at his work with the energy which was to mark his entire career. In *An Autobiographical Sketch* he wrote, "From the first day the business had a fascination for me. Time was all too short to accomplish what I was called upon to do. I frequently worked on Sundays and holidays. I began to make friends and sales."[1] In 1893 he was appointed manager of the firm's high school and college business in Chicago, moved to that city, and became a partner in 1894. He remained with the company for fifty-six years altogether, becoming chairman of the partnership in 1933, and first president and chairman of the board of the corporation in 1939. During this period he guided it through the great Depres-

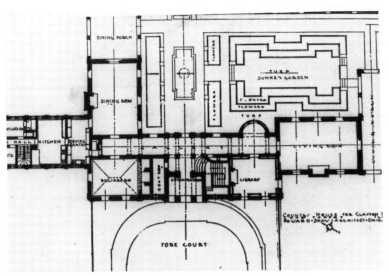

5. Mark house, plan, *Architectural Record,* vol. XLII, No. 6, December 1917

sion and numerous other vicissitudes; many of its successful authors were secured through his influence.

Hilton is a good example of the Shaw client who, on intellectual or professional grounds, wanted to build a city house near the University of Chicago. A close observer of the educational scene, he was a friend and admirer of President William Rainey Harper, and in his autobiography compares him with President Eliot of Harvard, somewhat to the latter's disadvantage. Hilton was always conscious of the sales possibilities of books written by the university's prestigious faculty. An amusing case in point is his experience with the famous archaeologist James Henry Breasted. For a long while, says Hilton, "Dr. Breasted declined to write the book that Ginn and Company urged, he was more interested in archeological excavating than in writing. But he lectured widely, on one occasion, for example, going from Chicago to Pittsburgh for the purpose. Ginn seized upon this to argue 'Two nights on the train, a thousand listeners. If you will make us a book, we promise you a daily audience of twenty-five to fifty thousand.' Breasted capitulated." [2] The result of this decision was *Ancient Times,* a best seller which came to the attention of John D. Rockefeller, Jr., and influenced him to endow the Oriental Institute. Obviously Hilton, like Shaw, moved easily in the academic atmosphere. The house which Shaw built for him at

6. Mark house, gallery, *Architectural Record,* vol. XLII, No. 6, December 1917

5640 Woodlawn Avenue, just a block from the Robie House, was large enough to accommodate himself, his wife, and six children, and later became the residence of the president of the university.

Although Hilton was essentially a city person, he shared many of the tastes of the North Shore Establishment. Tennis was one of his hobbies, and he played it well for many years; golf he never mastered. He liked bridge, and as a highly competitive individual, enjoyed facing competent opponents. A Mason as well as a member of the Union League, University, and Quadrangle Clubs and the Midlothian Country Club, he was devoted to the society of his fellows and in his memoirs observed that he would have missed much without his club life and the firm friendships which it brought him. Perhaps because of New England upbringing, he was probably more active in his church than most of Shaw's other clients. For twenty years he was chairman of the board of the Congregational church in Hyde Park, and each fall had the onerous task of arranging the balancing of its budget.

Hilton's prominence in the publishing world brought him three major opportunities to participate in national politics. During the First World War he served under Newton D. Baker as chief of the settlement division of the Student Army Train-

7. Mark house,
billiard room,
*Architectural
Record,* vol. XLII,
No. 6, December
1917

191

ing Corps. Later, in the nineteen twenties, he was a member of the Tax Simplification Board under Secretary of the Treasury Andrew Mellon; this was a board concerned with rectifying the inequities of the income tax, and it was, of course, heavily oriented toward the interests of business. Hilton was a director of two Chicago banks, so the work must have been quite congenial to him. Finally, during the early New Deal period he was chairman of the educational publishers code committee under the National Recovery Administration. As with the industrialist Robert Lamont, his connections with the world of government were excellent.

Hilton's real avocation, however, was service to his alma mater, Dartmouth College, and to various other educational institutions. Always an enthusiastic alumnus, he served as a trustee from 1905 to 1915, and his efforts were largely responsible for the spread of Dartmouth's popularity in the Midwest, which did much to transform it from a provincial New England school into a national institution. While a trustee he suggested the annual alumni subscription, which has grown into the outstandingly successful Dartmouth College Fund. Later he gave to Dartmouth its eighteen-hole golf course. Other educational institutions on whose boards he served were the Chicago Theological Seminary (1908–1946), Con-

8. Mark house, plaster ceiling in dining room, courtesy of Kenneth Krone

192

stantinople Women's College (1926) and Colby College (1930 –1940). He seems always to have been an active trustee. Before 1908 the Chicago Theological Seminary had been located on the west side of the city; as a member of its board he urged the move to a site adjacent to the University of Chicago, which was accomplished with much benefit to the school. In 1924, in memory of a deceased son, he gave to the seminary the Thorndike Hilton Memory Chapel, and in memory of another child he established the Ruth Sibley Hilton Music Foundation at Wellesley. When he joined the trustees of Colby College, its campus occupied cramped quarters next to the railroad tracks in Waterville, Maine; he was influential in moving the college to a new and more attractive location on Mayflower Hill outside the town. Not surprisingly, he collected honorary degrees from Colby and Dartmouth as well as from Northwestern. In his trusteeships he obviously displayed the same qualities of energy and prethought which made him a success in publishing.

Unhappily, no record of the relationship between Shaw and Hilton remains, but it is noteworthy that the house was preceded by a building for Ginn and Company on Prairie Avenue in 1907. In this instance the commercial building probably established the connection which led to the later domestic commission.

Pp. 207–209

1. Edward L.
Ryerson, courtesy
of Kaufmann and
Fabry Co.

193

Mr. and Mrs. Donald R. McLennan (Lake Forest, Illinois, 1914)

The life of Donald McLennan is a good illustration of the phenomenal expansion of the insurance business in twentieth-
century America. Born October 27, 1873, in Duluth, Minnesota, he attended high school and business college in that
city and began his career there as a bank clerk in 1888. Soon
thereafter he entered the insurance field, moving to Chicago
in 1905 to form the firm of Burrows, Marsh, and McLennan.
Today Marsh and McLennan continues to flourish and has
offices in New York, San Francisco, Minneapolis, and many
other cities. As with John P. Wilson, his excellent business
judgment caused his advice to be sought by many companies
in varied industrial and financial areas, some of them closely
linked to his early experience in northern Minnesota. In addition to his own firm, his directorships included the Common-
wealth Edison Company, Evergreen Mining Company, the
first National Bank of Lake Forest, Great Lakes Power Company, International Transit Company, Minnesota Sintering
Company, Montgomery Ward, North Range Iron Company,
Pullman Incorporated, Continental Chicago Corporation, Continental Illinois Bank and Trust Company, and the Empire
Securities Corporation—truly a formidable array.

In 1906 McLennan married Katherine Cole Noyes of Milwaukee. The house which Shaw built for them on North Lake

2. Ryerson house, garden facade, *Architectural Record,* vol. XXXIII, No. 4, April 1913

194

Road in Lake Forest was constructed in 1914. It had to be roomy and capable of expansion since the couple had a large family. A fourth child was on the way when they moved in, and two more followed. The choice of Shaw as architect was a simple matter since the McLennans had frequently seen his work and often saw him socially. He lived in the section of the suburb where they wanted to build, and they were certain that he would build a house perfectly satisfactory to their taste. In response to the question, "What do you think of the work of Frank Lloyd Wright?", Mrs. McLennan replied that she thought his houses were "perfectly awful" and looked like gas stations. Shaw, on the other hand "didn't do anything queer"; his houses were popular and never stood vacant for long.

As might be expected, the relationship with the architect was harmonious. Both husband and wife worked with Shaw on the project; Mrs. McLennan was in charge of the decoration. She characterizes herself as quite conservative in her taste; the only modern thing in the house is a small statue by Sylvia Shaw Judson, Shaw's daughter. Mrs. McLennan recalls Shaw with a great deal of admiration, calling him "a real gentleman, a wonder." One of his attractions for the affluent, she remarked, was that "he lived a nice life himself," and thus could easily understand the preferences of his clients. For example, he would never have built a house without adequate servants'

3. Ryerson house,
front doorway,
courtesy of
Wayne Andrews

quarters. In their own house Mrs. McLennan remembers giving in to Shaw on many points but adds that he also accommodated his plans to suit their requirements in many ways.

In their political and religious attitudes and in their recreations the McLennans were typical of the class to which they belonged. Their political affiliation was strongly Republican, and they attended the Presbyterian Church but were not particularly active. The children went to Sunday school; that was about all. Both enjoyed society, and Mr. McLennan belonged to a number of clubs in Chicago and Lake Forest. These included the Union League, Chicago, Mid-Day, Commercial, Old Elm, Attic, and Onwentsia. His closest friends were his business associates, and his major avocation was sailing. The house, however, should be seen primarily as a family-centered structure rather than as a backdrop for social activities.

Professor and Mrs. George E. Vincent (Chicago, Illinois, 1902)

Indicative of Shaw's close relationship with the University of Chicago was the house which he built for Professor and Mrs. George E. Vincent on University Avenue. Born at Rockford, Illinois, in 1864 into the family of a Methodist bishop, George Vincent graduated from Yale in 1885. For a few years thereafter he stayed in New Haven doing editorial work for the Chautauqua Press, and it was during this period that he met

4. Ryerson house, gallery, *Architectural Record,* vol. XXXIII, No. 4, April 1913

196

Shaw, who became a lifelong friend. Both, of course, were fellow Midwesterners confronting the strange new world of Eastern genteel culture. In 1892 Vincent returned to Chicago to accept a graduate fellowship in sociology at the new university on the Midway. Taking his doctorate in 1895, he rose rapidly in the academic hierarchy. A close friend of President William Rainey Harper, he was appointed dean of the junior colleges in 1900 and dean of the faculties of arts, literature, and science in 1907, remaining in that position until 1911, when he left to become president of the University of Minnesota. He stayed at Minnesota until 1916, when he was selected as president of the Rockefeller Foundation, which post he held until his retirement in 1929. In addition to these jobs Vincent was a member of the Commission for Relief in Belgium, chairman of a hospital survey in New York City, and a member of the United States delegation to the Pan-American Conference at Santiago, Chile, in 1923. In the fashion of his kind, Vincent collected numerous honorary degrees, lectured at foreign (Scandinavian) universities, and was a prolific, if not profound, writer. He was, in fact, a fine example of the educational administrator-philanthropoid with strong governmental connections, a type increasingly influential in American life today. Such men are apt to have significant influence on a good many architectural commissions, and it is a noteworthy fact

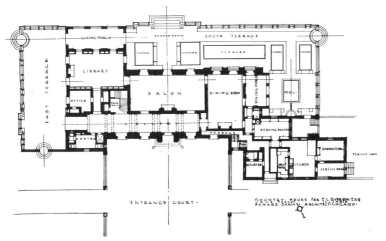

Country house for E.L. Ryerson Esq.
Howard Shaw, Architect, Chicago

5. Ryerson house, ground-floor plan, *Architectural Record,* vol. XXXIII, No. 4, April 1913

that a good many Shaw-designed structures sprang up in the neighborhood of the Vincent house.

As a member of the university community Vincent not surprisingly had leisure interests somewhat at variance with those of Shaw's businessmen clients. He read a great deal, loved the theater, attended frequently, and often entertained visiting actors, actresses, and producers. As a spokesman for the emerging discipline of sociology, Vincent was in demand as a speaker all over the country, and since both he and his wife enjoyed travel, these invitations were most welcome. The family recreations were apparently out-of-door life, camping, and mountain climbing rather than golf, sailing, or horseback riding. In spite of Vincent's family background they were not active in church work, although they did attend more or less regularly. Although Vincent was obviously a shrewd observer of the world and of men, it is not recorded that he, or his wife, ever showed any interest in politics. His political talents were apparently largely academic.

Mr. and Mrs. Clayton Mark (Lake Forest, Illinois, 1912)

Ills. pp. 185–192

The career of Clayton Mark is an illustration of the opportunities open to an energetic and talented newcomer in the Chicago business world of the late nineteenth century. Born at Fredericksburg, Pennsylvania, in 1858, Mark was educated in

6. Ryerson house,
entryway, *Archi-
tectural Record,*
vol. XXXIII, No. 4,
April 1913

198

the public schools of Pennsylvania and Chicago, and in 1876 went to work as a clerk with the Chicago Malleable Iron Company. In later years he was apparently always sensitive about his lack of formal education; his sons recall that he was a great reader, especially fond of Dickens, and that he took a leading role on the Chicago School Board. In 1880 Mark became secretary of Chicago Malleable Iron Company, and when the company's successor was organized as the National Malleable Castings Company, Mark became director of the Chicago works. Subsequently he was vice president and a member of the board for many years.

His real career, however, began in 1888 when he founded the Mark Manufacturing Company, a separate and independent firm for the fabrication and sale of water-well supplies. During his years with the older company Mark had noticed a huge potential market for well points (small castings used in the construction of wells), and he determined to supply this expanding need among the farmers of the Midwest. Within a few years he had enlarged the business to include the making of steel pipe; he built a pipe mill at Evanston and bought one at Zanesville, Ohio. In 1906 he formed the Vinegar Hill Zinc Company for the mining of zinc ores operating in the zinc fields of Illinois, Wisconsin, Kansas, and Oklahoma, and in 1914 the National Zinc Separating Company to roast zinc

7. Ryerson house,
dining room,
*Architectural
Record,* vol.
XXXIII, No. 4,
April 1913

199

ores. In the same period he established a system of jobbers to handle his products in the Midwest and California. All of these ventures came about as natural consequences of the initial decision to make well points. By 1916 he was ready to begin the erection of a self-contained steel mill at Indiana Harbor, Indiana, to supply his own requirements for raw steel. This plant had an annual capacity of about 450,000 tons of raw steel. An interesting feature of the Clayton Mark story is his decision *not* to engage in this end of the steel business and to sell the mill to Youngstown Sheet and Tube shortly after the First World War. He simply felt that this line of work was not a natural thing for his company.

During the nineteen twenties the Mark Manufacturing Company was again concerned with the fabrication of well supplies, pipe, and conduit, and its leadership began to search for a better way to make pipe. With the stimulus of the founder, Clayton Mark, Jr., and Wilfred Sykes invented the present method for the production of electrically welded tubing. The process was patented in 1928, and four years later the new tubing was offered to the public. Clayton Mark died in 1936, but the company which he founded continues to the present day with an excellent reputation for low-cost, high-quality products and expert salesmanship in a highly competitive field. As we review this history, the chief qualities which emerge

8. Ryerson house, library, *Architectural Record,* vol. XXXIII, No. 4, April 1913

are Clayton Mark's uncanny ability to anticipate demand and to be ready for it when it arrived. He saw the need for well points in an expanding agricultural economy. He acquired the necessary facilities to enable him to meet that demand. Though not technically skilled himself, he saw the need for new methods of production. He was the very model of the enterprising capitalist.

Needless to say, Clayton Mark worked very hard. His son remarks, "His hobby was his business," and adds that he even went so far as to have the mail brought out to him by motorcycle on Sundays. Notwithstanding this devotion to business, he contrived to take part in a phenomenal number of civic affairs. His chief interest was in public education. He was a member of the Chicago Board of Education for nine years and chairman of the finance committee for a long period which included the year 1902, when, by a sudden change in the law, the school tax was made $1,500,000 less than in the preceding year. From 1902 to 1905 he was president of the board. During his term of service he advocated freeing the superintendent of schools from political interference and placing with him the initiative in educational matters. He also advocated the appointment and promotion of teachers from a merit list. And these reforms were adopted. Furthermore, vacation schools were recognized as entitled to support from

Pp. 209–212

1. Gustavus Swift,
Jr., courtesy of
Swift & Co.

public funds; new school playgrounds were provided; schools for the deaf and blind were established; kindergartens were incorporated into the public school system; and technical high school work was extended. It should be noted that Mark's firm Republicanism (he was a Taft supporter all the way in 1912) did not prevent him from sponsoring educational innovations. In addition to his services on the Board of Education, Mark was president of the Civic Federation, one of the most active reform groups in the city from 1907 to 1909, and afterward served as a member of its executive committee. He was also a life member of the Chicago Historical Society and the Field Museum and a governing life member of the Art Institute, though there is no evidence that he ever took much interest in these institutions. In any event, the record is that of an individual with overwhelming energy and drive. Beside Clayton Mark, men like W. H. Winslow and Arthur Heurtley seem almost dreamy and introspective.

In 1912 the frame house where the Mark family were living in Lake Forest burned to the ground, and the occasion arose for a new dwelling. Clayton Mark knew Shaw through his good friend Louis Swift, who had already worked with the architect, and in any case Shaw by this time was well known in the community, so the connection is easily established. The two men got on well from the start, and four years later Mark asked

Shaw to design a model town in connection with his steel mill at Indiana Harbor. Like most such ventures, this was apparently not a success. The program for the house was a bit unusual in that it included accommodations for nine children, the largest number among the clients of either Wright or Shaw. The size of this family is perhaps an indication of sheer vitality and appetite for life, as it is today with the Kennedy clan. The design of the building went smoothly, and the original plan was changed only slightly by Mrs. Mark, who asked that the bedrooms face east to overlook the lake rather than west as originally planned. A Chicago decorator named Nielson was responsible for the furnishing, although Mark himself picked out several paintings from the Anderson Art Gallery, including a large Inness, which today hangs in the company offices. He also picked out several fine Oriental rugs. As with most of Shaw's clients, his taste in art was conservative. Neither he nor his wife took much interest in the construction, which apparently ran somewhat over budget. This excess cost was no particular problem and doesn't appear to have bothered the owner. Like the Wilson house, it was an exceptional job of building, using a good deal of reinforced concrete.

Despite the size of the structure, it is not to be construed as a setting for lavish entertainments. The Marks were apparently

3. Swift house, front entrance, the *Spur,* April 1, 1919

203

a close-knit family which did not carry on an extensive social life. Mark enjoyed reading to his children before dinner, and there were a good many family games. While he played golf and belonged to the Shore Acres, Old Elm, and Onwentsia Clubs, his major recreation was in his civic work. In addition to the posts which we have already enumerated, he was a trustee of Lake Forest Academy and president of the board of trustees of the Civic Opera building in Chicago. Finally, the Marks were members of the Presbyterian Church in Lake Forest. After the death of his wife in 1915, Mark did not remarry.

Mr. and Mrs. Benjamin E. Bensinger (Glencoe, Illinois, 1908)

Benjamin E. Bensinger was born at Louisville, Kentucky, in 1868, the son of Moses and Eleanor (Brunswick) Bensinger, and it was in that city that he received most of his primary education. After coming to Chicago at the age of seventeen, he attended high school there and took a short commercial course at the Bryant and Stratton Business College. "From his earliest studies," says a biographer, "he manifested an unusual grasp of practical affairs of the day"; [3] that grasp was to carry him to the very top of the business ladder.

His academic work over, Bensinger went to work as office boy for Brunswick-Balke-Collender, the firm founded by his grandfather. During the three years that he remained with

4. Swift house,
entrance hall, the
Spur, April 1, 1919

that company he observed its methods so carefully that he was able to make a real contribution to the Bensinger Self-Adding Cash Register Company, his father's firm, which he joined in 1888. When that concern went out of business in 1890, he returned to Brunswick, and thereafter was promoted rapidly in the organization, becoming first vice president and a member of the board in 1903. In this capacity he was able to exert real influence on the management of the company, and when his father died a year later, he was made president, a job which he held for most of the rest of his life. When Bensinger took charge of Brunswick-Balke-Collender, it was already the world's largest manufacturer of billiard and pocket tables, bowling supplies, bar fixtures, and general cabinet work, with factories located in the largest cities of the United States. His achievement was to push the company into the manufacture of phonographs, radios, records, and the associated devices demanded by the burgeoning entertainment industry. As the popularity of the new machines grew, the company's profits increased accordingly. Like Clayton Mark in an entirely different field, he saw the potential of the market and rose to the challenge.

In 1908 Mr. and Mrs. Bensinger (the former Rose Frank of Chicago) decided to build a house in the North Shore suburb

5. Swift house, living room, the *Spur,* April 1, 1919

of Glencoe. In this instance it was probably the wife who approached Shaw, since the husband was too busy with the company. While Shaw was not as well known in the Chicago Jewish community as his slightly older contemporary Jens Jensen, he had an excellent reputation; among his commissions were houses for Morris Rosenwald, Louis B. Kuppenheimer, Robert Schaffner, and A. G. Becker, as well as the Lake Shore Country Club in Glencoe, so it is not surprising that the Bensingers went to him. As usual with Shaw, the design and construction of the house went smoothly. The budget was $25,000, Shaw kept within it, and for years afterward the Bensingers spoke of him with the highest regard. Mrs. Bensinger handled the furnishings.

In their leisure-time activities the Bensingers were typical of the North Shore Establishment. Mr. Bensinger rode horseback, and played golf and billiards, while his wife was active in a variety of civic groups. A thoroughly sociable individual, he belonged to the City, Collegiate, Illinois Athletic, and Standard Clubs in Chicago, and to the Lake Shore Country Club, which last was located not far from his house. Among his good friends were the advertising man A. D. Lasker and the philanthropist Julius Rosenwald, and with these gentlemen he occasionally joined in a game of poker. His wife was the center

of the family gatherings; she liked to write poetry and short stories, not professionally but for the amusement of her children and intimate friends. At parties she created a festive atmosphere with costumes, games, and so on, and her son recalls her as a humorous woman, spirited and gay. While neither husband nor wife could be called devout or observant in the traditional sense, Bensinger was certainly prominent in the affairs of Chicago's Jewish community. Connected with the Associated Jewish Charities since his early years, he was president in 1917, bringing to the job the same energy which he showed in his own business. He was also secretary of Mount Sinai Synagogue.

Though certainly Republican, the Bensingers were probably somewhat more liberal than most of the other Shaw clients. Both were Theodore Roosevelt enthusiasts, but there is no record of how they voted in the year of crisis, 1912. More significantly, they were very fond of travel and went to Europe at least once a year. These trips made them very conscious of world affairs, and were also, in Bensinger's opinion, important for the education of his children; not possessing a college education himself, he took a close personal interest in this matter. It is perhaps hardly necessary to say that his two sons went into the family firm. Here, as so often among the Shaw clients, we encounter a strong dynastic feeling.

7. Swift house, up-
stairs hall, the
Spur, April 1, 1919

207

Ills. pp. 193–200

Edward L. Ryerson (Lake Forest, 1906 and 1912)

Like many of Shaw's clients Edward L. Ryerson was a second
generation Chicagoan. Born in the city in 1854, he was the son
of Joseph T. Ryerson, who founded the famous steel manufacturing firm. A graduate of Yale's Sheffield Scientific School
in 1876, he returned to Chicago to go into the family business,
in 1878 became a junior partner, and in 1883 succeeded his
father as head of the company. Under his leadership Ryerson
Steel developed into the largest independent producer in the
nation with a plant covering more than sixteen acres in Chicago. It manufactured structural, plate, and sheet steel, and
more than one thousand specialties, and is today an important
division of the present Inland Steel Corporation. Unlike many
of his contemporaries, Ryerson does not appear to have collected directorships in other companies. Except for membership on the executive committee of the Illinois Merchants
Trust, he reserved his business energies for his own company,
of which he was president until 1912, when he became chairman of the board.

In civic affairs Ryerson was president of the Newberry Library from 1914 until his death in 1928, and trustee and vice
president of St. Luke's Hospital and of the Chicago Historical
Society. He was also a member of the Art Institute and of the
University, City, Chicago (president), Casino, Saddle and Cycle,

8. Swift house, dining room, the *Spur*, April 1, 1919

and Wayfarers Clubs, and of the Onwentsia, Shore Acres, and Old Elm Country Clubs. While he evidently enjoyed these organizations, his major relaxation was unquestionably the building, furnishing, and landscaping of two large houses in Lake Forest, both designed by Howard Van Doren Shaw. The first of these dates from 1906 and the second from 1912. Ryerson's interest in architecture was, according to his son, due primarily to his interest in landscape architecture. At one time he and a group of friends formed a foundation to provide fellowships for students in that field. Today these funds have been transferred to the University of Illinois, which continues to provide traveling fellowships in architecture and landscape design to qualified graduates of that school. These awards are known as the Edward L. Ryerson grants. It therefore seems probable that the reason for the building of the second dwelling so soon after the completion of the first was simply that the grounds of the first did not give him sufficient scope for the construction of landscape gardens, a hobby which he pursued with real enthusiasm. The gardens of the second Ryerson place were designed by Jens Jensen, and they were among the most extensive which that great artist built on the North Shore. Ryerson took a close personal interest in them, even going so far as to import pieces of sculpture from Italy especially for their adornment. Clearly he wanted a showplace, and

Pp. 212–214

1. Robert P. Lamont, courtesy of Chicago Historical Society

in terms of the taste of the time, he certainly got one. The Ryerson house and gardens were twice published, and much admired in the best society.

In manner Ryerson appears to have been a classic example of the imperious nineteenth-century tycoon. "Under an exterior of reserve," says an official biography, "Mr. Ryerson sought to conceal an exceedingly generous nature." [4] More to the point is the remark of one of Shaw's daughters that of all his clients, Edward Ryerson was the only one who ever frightened her father. Since Shaw was accustomed to dealing with men of wealth and power, this is a revealing comment. We also know that Jens Jensen, who had a far stormier personality than the mild-mannered and charming Shaw, had great difficulties with Ryerson. In the course of a shouting match with his client, he even threatened to walk off the job. It is perhaps suggestive that both Ryerson houses are very formal and Italianate, much more so than most of Shaw's work, and that Jensen built for him one of the few formal gardens which he ever designed. Edward Ryerson must have been a formidable man.

Mr. and Mrs. Gustavus Swift, Jr. (Chicago, 1913)

Ills. pp. 201–208

Mr. and Mrs. Gustavus Swift, Jr., may be considered as typical of the packing-house aristocracy for whom Shaw did several

2. Lamont house, front elevation, courtesy of Kenneth Krone

large houses. He was one of the sons of Gustavus Swift, who founded Swift and Company, and while not so important in the affairs of the company as his elder brother Louis, his outlook was representative of his circle. It may be noted that these packing families tended to intermarry and to live reasonably close to each other on the south side of the city. Thus Edward Morris, head of Morris & Company, married one of the sisters of Gustavus Swift, Jr., and lived in a Shaw-designed mansion on Drexel Boulevard, while the Swifts themselves built on Astor Street. Arthur Meeker, whose father was a packer, recalls that so many of his relatives lived near him on Prairie Avenue that the area was known as "Meekerville." In these circumstances it is easy to see how a string of commissions resulted from Shaw's first contact with the group, which may have been with Morris or with Arthur Leonard, president of the Union Stock Yards.

Like Edward Ryerson, Gustavus Swift was a second generation Chicagoan. Born in 1881, he did not, like Ryerson, go east to school, but entered the family firm directly from the public schools of the city. In general, the packers seem to have placed less emphasis on higher education than the other commercial groups in the city. Leonard and Morris were also without college degrees. We should immediately add that the lack of a B.A. was no deterrent to success in the packing business. Be-

sides running their own firms, both men held several directorships in other concerns and were counted among the most
influential men in the business community. Swift, too, was a
man whose advice was widely sought.

The Swift house was built in 1913 to accommodate husband, wife, and four growing children, plus two or three servants. Mrs. Swift recalls that Shaw paid particular attention to
the needs of the children, and adds that she and her husband
shared equally in the planning of the house. She also remembers that they knew Shaw socially and says that it was a "very
natural thing" to think of him when one was going to build a
house. Despite its size, the house was conceived primarily as
a backdrop for family life. While the Swifts unquestionably
knew the leading families of Chicago, they did not entertain
a great deal. Mr. Swift was devoted to his job as vice president
of Swift and Company, and for relaxation played golf and
bridge. His wife was an equally ardent golfer and bridge player,
and in addition enjoyed the concerts of the Chicago Symphony. They were members of the Onwentsia, Midlothian, and
South Shore Country Clubs, and of several clubs in the city as
well. They were not interested in the Art Institute and do not
seem to have been particularly active in civic organizations.
They were simply a typical upper-class family of large means,
and today Mrs. Swift speaks of the job which Shaw did for

them in glowing terms. At the time they built she had never heard of Frank Lloyd Wright.

Ills. pp. 209–214

Mr. and Mrs. Robert P. Lamont (Lake Forest, 1924)

"In that vast American enterprise known as the steel industry," said the editor of *Chicago and Its Makers,* "no one is better known nor more outstanding than Robert Patterson Lamont." [5] The career of this man is, indeed, a superb example of the success attainable by a newcomer in the Chicago business world of the early twentieth century.

Born in Detroit in 1867, Lamont secured his primary and high school education in the public schools of that city. Having had since his earliest youth an inclination for engineering studies, he entered the nearby University of Michigan and was graduated in 1891 with a Bachelor of Science in Civil Engineering. His Chicago career began almost immediately after his college training, for in 1892 he was chosen as one of the engineers of the famous World's Columbian Exposition. At this time his ability caught the attention of Shailer and Schnigkau, a contracting firm which was responsible for many of the fair's buildings. He joined them as an engineer and later was admitted to membership in the firm as secretary. In 1897 he took a position as first vice president with the Simplex Rail-

213

way Appliance Company, which had been organized by William V. Kelley, another Shaw client. He occupied this post for the next eight years and then resigned to take the job of vice president of the American Steel Foundry, with which company he was to be associated for the remainder of his career. He became president in 1912 and in that post oversaw its expansion during the war years.

So brilliant was his executive ability and so good was his business judgment that he was soon called upon to assume directorships in a number of other leading corporations. These included the First National Bank of Chicago, Montgomery Ward and Company, International Harvester, the American Radiator Company, Armour and Company, the *Chicago Daily News,* Illinois Bell Telephone, and Dodge Brothers, the automobile manufacturing concern. He was also chairman of the board of Griffin Wheel Company. He seems to have been rather a prototype of Sidney Weinberg, the New Yorker who probably holds the modern record for directorships. It is notable that none of his positions involved the solution of engineering problems as such. His engineering background undoubtedly helped him, but his success was a result of executive ability and sound business judgment.

In the First World War he took time out from his career to

6. Lamont house, hallway, courtesy of Kenneth Krone

go to Washington. In February 1918, he was commissioned a major, and in October of that year he was appointed chief of the procurement division of the Ordnance Department and promoted to colonel. With his background in industry, this job was, of course, a natural one.

On the social side Lamont was a member of the Chicago, Union League, University, and Mid-Day Clubs. He relaxed by playing golf at the Shore Acres and Old Elm Country Clubs. At his home in Lake Forest he had a notable collection of etchings. His family life seems to have been unexceptionable. In any case his wife and three children must have taken second place to his business career, which was climaxed with his appointment as Secretary of Commerce in the Hoover Administration. When that Administration left office, he became president of the American Iron and Steel Institute from 1932 to 1934 and shortly thereafter retired.

Mr. and Mrs. Walter Stanton Brewster (Lake Forest, 1920)
Mr. and Mrs. Walter S. Brewster were typical of the society group in Chicago whose main interest was the Art Institute. Numbering Elder Brewster and John Robinson of *Mayflower* fame among his ancestors, Brewster was the son of a prosperous investment broker in the city who was able to send

Pp. 217–220

1. Candid photo in 1912 of Mr. and Mrs. Prentiss Coonley and Lawrence Armour — courtesy of Chicago Historical Society

215

him to St. Paul's School and Yale, from which he graduated in 1895. Returning to the vital Chicago of the post-World-Fair period, he entered the office of Edward L. Brewster and Company at a salary of forty dollars a month, and in due course rose to a partnership and its accompanying affluence. One feels, however, that the acquisition of money was never a major objective of Brewster's life. On the contrary, there are strong indications of public service and aesthetic interest as his chief motivations.

Once he had attained business success, Brewster turned to the affairs of his city. He became a trustee of the Art Institute and also of the American Academy in Rome, and he devoted much time to both these institutions. Like many Chicagoans of his class, Brewster traveled to Europe frequently and was able to visit the Academy several times. He was also president of the Foundation for Architecture and Landscape Architecture, which did a good deal to improve the physical appearance of Chicago at various times. Long interested in charitable organizations, he was a director of the United Charities of Chicago for many years, and in the years 1925–1928 he was its president. From 1921 to 1923 he was president of the Chicago Stock Exchange. Of an extremely sociable disposition, the Brewsters belonged to many clubs. These included the

2. Coonley house,
front elevation,
courtesy of
Richard Nickel

216

Chicago, University, Saddle and Cycle, Racquet, Casino, Cliff Dwellers, and Onwentsia, and in New York, the Racquet and Tennis, and Grolier Clubs.

Mrs. Brewster, the former Kate Lancaster, was one of the most brilliant hostesses of her day in Chicago. Arthur Meeker, who knew her well, remarks that she was

. . . a talented creature with such a diversity of gifts that one hardly knows where to begin to praise. (The bad fairies gave her only one, the inability to be content with what she had.) Her work for France in two world wars brought her international honours; at home she was admired for an impeccable taste that was all her own; she had no need, unlike most women of wealth and position to acquire it from others. An authority on gardening, she wrote a book on it, her collection of modern pictures was famous; her houses both in town and in the country, were beautiful but livable museums. . . . Kate was pretty, too; not even looks had been denied her. In youth her poetic blue eyes and fragile air suggested a forget-me-not, a nymph by Greuze, or anything else you like that's delicately seductive. This fragility was deceiving; she had a will of steel.[6]

Since Brewster himself was, on the basis of his pictures, a tall distinguished-appearing person, they must have been an extraordinarily handsome couple. Meeker adds that their parties were notable for the perfection of their food, flower arrangements, and table appointments. He even suspected that their women friends saved their most attractive gowns to

3. Coonley house,
garden facade,
courtesy of
Richard Nickel

wear to the Brewsters'. An evening at their house must have
been a remarkable experience.

Mr. and Mrs. Prentiss Loomis Coonley (Lake Forest, 1908)

Ills. pp. 215–220

Born in Chicago in 1880, Prentiss L. Coonley was the son of
John Clark and Lydia Avery Coonley. After preparation at the
Chicago Latin School, he went east to college, taking his B.A.
at Harvard in 1903. Returning to the city, he immediately
associated himself with the family manufacturing firm, as
well as with a number of other similar, smaller concerns, notably the Walworth Manufacturing Company, the Nugent Steel
Castings Company, and the Electric Steel Company. Coming
from a background of inherited wealth like many of Shaw's
other clients, he did not have to work, but gave no thought
to becoming a gentleman of leisure. Evidently his work was
of an engineering type, and in later years he often regretted
that he had not had an engineering education. He often said
that he had a very good time at Harvard but didn't get much
else out of his experience there.

In 1905 Coonley married Alice Lord of Chicago, and in 1908
asked Howard Van Doren Shaw to design a house in Lake Forest for his family, which consisted of himself, his wife, and two
small daughters. The fascinating question immediately arises:

218

Why did Prentiss Coonley go to Shaw for his house at the same time his brother was approaching Frank Lloyd Wright? The answer to this query is not easy to perceive. Miss Eleanor Coonley remarks that Shaw was a well-known architect in Chicago at the time and believes that her parents knew him socially. It is certainly true that the Coonleys and Shaws belonged to some of the same clubs, notably the University and Onwentsia (Coonley also belonged to the Chicago, Casino, Racquet, and Attic). It is also noteworthy that the Coonley house is located on Green Bay Road, in close proximity to the Shaw residence. Eleanor Coonley spent a good deal of time there and became a good friend of the Shaw family, especially of daughter Theodora. She recalls the household as a lively one, where something was always going on.

On a somewhat deeper level we may note that Prentiss Coonley was evidently a somewhat more extroverted and outgoing personality than his older brother. He was always more interested in managing the family business than Avery, who actually withdrew from it to devote most of his time to work for the Christian Science Church. Indeed, Avery's interest in religion may have been for him the slightly offbeat characteristic which he shared with so many of the other Wright clients. As we have remarked elsewhere, most of them were, in one way or another, marginal to the middle-class society of their

day. Prentiss Coonley, on the other hand, was a thoroughly conventional Episcopalian.

In politics Prentiss Coonley shared with his brother an un- usual liberality and breadth of outlook. His daughter com- ments that he was "one of the most unrepublican of Republi- cans," a man capable of entertaining all sorts of ideas and very open to divergent points of view. During the New Deal he moved to Washington and took a position with the N.R.A. Somewhat later he became one of the first members of the Business Advisory Council. He was, so far as can be seen, the only Shaw client with such a record.

For recreation the Coonley family did a good deal of horse- back riding. It will be remembered that Avery Coonley was also fond of this pastime, but he never pursued it with the enthusi- asm of his brother. Prentiss Coonley played polo and was, for a time, Master of the Onwentsia Hunt. In addition, he played the piano occasionally, and his wife was an avid gardener. They did a fair amount of entertaining, and here again they are different from the Avery Coonleys, who, despite the size of their house, very seldom had company. In comparison with her sister-in-law, Alice Coonley seems to have been a rather conventional person. She had none of Queene Ferry Coonley's interest in religion or in the arts, but preferred to spend most of her time with her children or her neighbors. It was, after all,

220

Mrs. Avery Coonley who first went to Wright, after seeing an ex-
hibition of his work at the Chicago Architectural Club. This fact
may be the key to the entire Coonley problem.

Ills. pp. 221–226 ### Mr. and Mrs. John P. Wilson (Chicago, 1924)

John P. Wilson was one of the most successful members of the
Chicago Bar. Born in the city in 1877, he was sent east to St.
Paul's School in Concord, New Hampshire, graduating from
that well-known institution in 1896. He went on to Williams
College, matriculating with the class of 1900, and to the Harvard Law School, where he took his LL.B. degree in 1903. Returning to Chicago in that year, he joined the law firm founded
by his father, an equally distinguished attorney, and within a
few years rose to prominence in the legal community. Wilson,
McIlvaine, Hale, and Templeton were personal attorneys for
many of the leaders among the city's business aristocracy,
and they handled wills, trusts, and if the need arose, divorces
and suits for alienation of affections. The Fields, McCormicks,
Swifts, and Armours found that his discretion and ability
could be relied upon, and in time he became a director of
International Harvester and Marshall Field. His trust work
brought him into close contact with the securities market, and
he also became a director of the Harris Trust and Savings, the
United Trust of New York, and the First National Bank of Chi-

Pp. 220–223

1. John P. Wilson,
courtesy of Chi-
cago Historical
Society

221

cago. Clearly, Wilson's judgment was valued by the financial leaders of the city.

Like many attorneys and businessmen of his generation, Wilson was a phenomenally hard worker. A member of his family states that his usual hours were 8 to 6, Monday through Saturday. He had, in fact, what might be called a dynastic sense; he worked to carry on the tradition of his father and to make a place for his son. He found time, however, to be a trustee of the University of Chicago and of the Newberry Library as well as president of the Children's Memorial Hospital. In addition, Wilson was what the period called "a good club man"; his fondness for the company of his fellows was evinced by memberships in the University, Mid-Day, Attic, Saddle and Cycle, Old Elm, Casino, Indian Hill, and Racquet Clubs. He liked golf, but his favorite recreation was sailing. In his later years he took his vacations aboard a Malabar class boat on Lake Michigan.

The second Mrs. Wilson, whom he married in 1916, shared his taste for society, and the house which they built in 1924 at 1516 North State Parkway may be seen primarily as the backdrop for an active social life. According to her stepson, Mrs. Wilson had originally wanted "an important classical Georgian house," but was very happy with Shaw's design. The probable source of the commission was Clay Judson, a Wilson law

partner who was married to one of Shaw's daughters, and it must have been one of the architect's last major domestic commissions in the city, since it was finished in the year of his death. Both husband and wife worked closely with Shaw. Wilson had been involved in a number of downtown real estate transactions, and though no engineer, was familiar with the building business, and took a close personal interest in the construction of his dwelling. The house was framed in concrete, a material which Shaw used frequently but made no effort to express in architectural terms. In later years Wilson used to joke that he had the lowest fire insurance rate in the city. The difficulty, of course, was that when later owners wished to remodel, they found it almost impossible to do so. In contrast to many of Wright's prairie houses, which were all too often badly constructed, most of Shaw's works were exceedingly solid. This, of course, was partly a question of cost and partly a matter of conservative versus radical (and sometimes unsound) building technology. As Barry Byrne has said, Wright had an almost naïve faith in a 2-by-4-inch stud.

For the furnishing of the home Mrs. Wilson had complete responsibility. According to a close friend she had a considerable knowledge of the English eighteenth century, and was determined to make her interior an authentic period piece. The Wilsons even made a special trip abroad to buy

3. Wilson house, entryway, courtesy of the *Western Architect,* September 1926

223

furniture, chiefly Chippendale and Sheraton. As one views old photographs of the living room, which stretched all the way across the house, he will certainly feel that she succeeded. The excellent collection of Lowestoft is especially notable.

In short, the Wilsons were a representative Chicago upper-class couple. The budget of their house was ample, the house was built well within it, and their relationship with the architect was excellent throughout. Subsequently the Wilson firm handled the legal details of Shaw's estate. Aside from the cares of the law office and of household management, the Wilsons found their major recreation in an active social life, and for that life Howard Van Doren Shaw provided a gracious and dignified setting.

Mr. and Mrs. Charles Stinson Pillsbury (Minneapolis, 1922)

Born in Minneapolis in 1878, Charles S. Pillsbury came of a family which has long been prominent in the flour-milling business and in the politics of Minnesota. His great-uncle was three times governor of the state, and his father founded the family milling concern, which is today the second largest in the United States. Taking his B.S. degree at the University of Minnesota in 1900, Pillsbury went immediately into the business. In 1908 he helped to reorganize the firm; in 1909 he became a director, and in 1910 vice president, which job he

held until his retirement in 1932. While Pillsbury does not appear to have been as important in the business as his twin brother, John Sargent, he still played a significant role in its expansion. In addition, he was president of the Sargent Land Company and the Keewatin Mining Company, vice president of the Real Estate Title Insurance Company, Sutton Land Company, and Meriden Iron Company, and secretary-treasurer of the Pillsbury Lumber Company. His directorships included the First National Bank of Minneapolis, the Kearsarge Land Company, Munsingwear Corporation of Milwaukee, the St. Paul and Sault Ste. Marie Railroad, and Vassar Company of Chicago. Some of these positions suggest the family interests in iron-ore lands in northern Minnesota; others are indicative of its importance in the financial life of the Twin Cities.

Perhaps because of their New England background, the Pillsburys have always been public-spirited. It was typical of this member of the clan that he took a leading role in the organization of the Pillsbury Settlement House, an institution which tried to do for Minneapolis approximately what Hull House had done for Chicago. He was also a generous contributor to the support of the Minneapolis Symphony Orchestra and a frequent attender of its concerts. For his other recreation he rode horseback, and somewhat surprisingly, was an amateur pilot. He learned to fly in 1915 and continued his

5. Wilson house, dining room, courtesy of the *Western Architect,* September 1926

225

interest in aviation for the rest of his life. During the First World War he served under the Assistant Secretary of War as an inspector of aviation training fields. In religion he was a Congregationalist, and in politics, it is hardly necessary to add, a Republican.

The source of the commission which Shaw received from Pillsbury to build a country house at Lake Minnetonka is a bit hard to determine. Although he was a member of the Chicago and University Clubs, he did not visit the city often. By the early nineteen twenties, however, Shaw had already done two dwellings in Minneapolis, a country house in 1909 for the grain broker Walter Douglas, who was lost on the *Titanic,* and a city place for the lumberman C. C. Bovey in 1912. Pillsbury may have been impressed by these. In any event, the program called for a country house on a rolling point of land jutting out into Lake Minnetonka, just to the west of the city. The property had been in the family for some time, and the new dwelling was to replace an older house which had burned down. It was to utilize the existing foundations and some of the same basement rooms, drains, and water system. There was also a ready-made garden plan by Edmund Phelps, a local landscape architect. Shaw liked the site immensely, and came up to Minneapolis several times to confer with the Pillsburys. Together they decided on an Italian farmhouse style for the new

6. Wilson house, fireplace, courtesy of the *Western Architect,* September 1926

226

building. It is interesting to note that this dwelling has recently been replaced by a contemporary house commissioned by Philip Pillsbury, son of Charles and recently retired president of Pillsbury Mills. The furnishing of Shaw's structure was largely the responsibility of Mrs. Pillsbury, who was assisted by a close friend who was also an interior decorator and furniture buyer. Many of the pieces came from France and Italy.

Charles Pillsbury was, then, a good example of the provincial magnate, a type who recurs several times in Shaw's clientele. In his tastes and general outlook on life he unquestionably resembled the members of the North Shore Establishment.

5 Footnotes

[1] Henry H. Hilton, *An Autobiographical Sketch* (North Tewksbury, Mass., 1947), p. 21.
[2] Henry H. Hilton, *Observations and Memories* (North Tewksbury, Mass., 1947), p. 57.
[3] Paul Gilbert and Charles Lee Bryson, *Chicago and Its Makers* (Chicago, 1929), p. 986.
[4] *National Cyclopedia of American Biography* (New York, 1931), p. 394.
[5] Gilbert and Bryson, *Chicago,* p. 924.
[6] Arthur Meeker, *Chicago With Love* (New York, 1955), p. 247.

6 The Failure of the Siege

We are now in a position to give a more general consideration to the Wrightian revolution. It is clear that by 1917 the powerful impulse which had produced the prairie houses, and the almost equally interesting work of Purcell and Elmslie, Walter Burley Griffin, and a number of others, was finished. Commenting on the exhibit of the Chicago Architectural Club in that year, Thomas Tallmadge wrote:

What is even more to be regretted is the absence of any evidence that the "Chicago School" as a potent style of architecture, any longer exists . . . clients, the wives of whom at least have received their architectural education in magazines edited in Boston and New York, now have turned back to pretty Colonial or fashionable Italian. . . . Where are Sullivan, Wright, Griffin, and the others? The absence of the work of these men has removed from the show the last vestige of local color.[1]

This passage is an excellent clue to the condition of architectural patronage at the time and, indeed, suggests one major reason for the collapse of the Prairie School. It calls attention to the importance of the shelter magazines in the story, a point which has recently been made with considerable vigor by Allen Brooks.[2] There were, however, as in all complex historical situations, a number of factors at work.

We have seen that the ideal Wright client couple tended to be members of a particular segment of the middle class. Very often the man was of an inventive turn of mind, or at any rate technologically oriented. If he had a college degree, it would ordinarily be in engineering from a Midwestern state university. Somewhere in the family musical ability was likely to exist. The wives tended to be active, vigorous women, devoted to their families and to community affairs. If they had an interest in reform, it was probably in the suffrage movement. Barry Byrne, who was in the Wright office for five years, remarks that "the clients had this in common: a healthy independence of mind with regard to the conventional."[3] We have attempted to analyze the sources of this independence. Now the question becomes, What happened to this group? Did this type of middle-class American suddenly cease to exist? This is hardly credible.

The answer appears to be that a number of things happened to make these people shift their attitude in regard to domestic architecture. As Brooks has pointed out, the magazines which the wives of potential clients read devoted more and more space to the various revivals and less to the architecture of the Prairie School. In this connection it is useful to consider briefly the case of *House Beautiful,* which was probably then the single most important periodical in the field.

In the United States prior to the First World War there were two leading magazines in what would today be called "the shelter field." The first was *House and Garden.* Founded in

229

1903 at Philadelphia, its point of view was always conservative. It espoused the traditional in architecture, in landscape, and in interior decoration. The second was *The House Beautiful,* founded in Chicago in 1896, and purchased the next year by Herbert S. Stone, son of a wealthy Chicago banker. While still a Harvard undergraduate, Stone had joined with Ingalls Kimball to put out a pioneering little magazine, *The Chap-Book,* and a bit later had formed the firm of Stone and Kimball, which published such important modern authors as Paul Verlaine and Stéphane Mallarmé. By 1896 Kimball wanted to move to New York, and so Stone sold his share of the business to his partner, and himself stayed behind in Chicago to run the *Chap-Book.* That periodical, says Frank Luther Mott, "though undeniably a *succes d'estime,* showed no signs of yielding a financial profit, and so in 1897 Stone purchased *The House Beautiful* and the next year disposed of the *Chap-Book* to the Chicago *Dial* in order to devote himself to publishing and editing the new magazine." [4] The task proved to be one for which he was admirably fitted. A man of great discrimination and artistic perception, he made *House Beautiful* (the slight change in title was effected in 1925) an outstanding advocate of good design. Moreover, he made it pay. By 1904 the circulation had reached 20,000, with a corresponding increase in the advertising section. Attractively illustrated and well edited, the magazine reached a significant portion of the great American middle class. Most important for this analysis, it gave substantial coverage to the works of the prairie architects and especially Wright. For example, in June, July, and August 1906, the lead article in each issue was devoted to Wright's work, and the verdicts were enthusiastic. The Hardy house in Racine had "an almost classic style and dignity," although it cost under $6000. Similar encomiums were accorded to the Glasner house in Glencoe and the De Rhodes house in South Bend, Indiana.

In 1910 the magazine's basic financial and management structure began to change and not in a way calculated to give the advocates of prairie architecture any hope or comfort. In that year a merger with *Modern Homes* of Memphis brought in new management. Stone remained as editor and retained at least a minority interest, but in 1911 an even more ominous event occurred: the magazine moved its offices to New York. This action was in keeping with the general shift of the publishing industry, a movement which was to have great cultural consequences for the entire nation. By 1920 New York was the major market for every product of the literary, visual, and musical imagination in America; being a success in the United States meant having a success in New York. This attitude was fatal to the prairie architects, who had flourished on a healthy

230

diet of regionalism. It meant that their rather rugged individuality was simply ignored as American culture became more and more homogenized. Perhaps it might be mentioned here that not until 1959 did Frank Lloyd Wright do a building in New York City.

During the next few years the management of *House Beautiful* underwent further changes, but these need not concern us here. Stone stayed on as editor until 1913, when he was succeeded by Virginia Robie, a veteran staff member with much the same point of view, who stayed on until 1915. We must note, however, that by the end of 1912 references to Wright had dwindled to a single uncaptioned picture of the Hickox house at Kankakee. It was used to illustrate the combination of plaster and wood. And while publications of prairie houses diminished, presentations of English country homes and French chateaux swelled to the proportions of a flood. It is no wonder that the Chicago architects felt that the national spirit was being infected by the deadly virus of the "Bozart" (to use H. L. Mencken's word). In other periodicals the story is similar. In 1910 *Country Life in America,* hitherto an advocate of the simple pastoral life of the old republic, carried a long article on "The Italian Villa," and thereafter gave little space to the prairie architects. The last mention was in the January 1914 issue, which reviewed a house in Seattle which was apparently done by Andrew Willatsen, who spent several years in Wright's office and absorbed much of his style. In the next few years the magazine showed a marked increase in colonial and European designs. Potential clients were thus subjected to a formidable publicity campaign mounted by the advocates of eclecticism.

In addition, by the time of the First World War they were confronted by a large body of work accomplished by sophisticated revivalists such as Shaw. In 1900 this work did not exist in quantity, and in 1908 or 1909 what there was of it might have reasonably been compared with the production of Wright and his contemporaries. By 1917, however, Shaw's key commissions, notably the second Ryerson house, had been finished, and were in full use and at the height of their fame. To the Ryerson house must, of course, be added the enormous place done by Arthur Heun for Ogden Armour at Lake Forest, and many others of like quality. Eclecticism now had the official stamp of approval of the North Shore Establishment and was therefore an enormously difficult movement to resist.

In this connection it is interesting to note that if we survey the Shaw clients after 1920, we find several individuals of a type who might, ten or fifteen years earlier, have gone to Wright. Mr. and Mrs. Morse Dell Plain were such a couple. Born in New Orleans in 1880, Dell Plain attended Syracuse University, where he took a degree in electrical engineering in 1903.

Following employment with Westinghouse Electric as a salesman, he became a power engineer for the Syracuse Lighting Company from 1909 to 1918, and in the latter year moved to northern Indiana, where he went to work for the United Gas Improvement Company, which was subsequently taken over by Samuel Insull and renamed the Northern Indiana Public Service Company. His career was thus essentially similar to that of Edwin Cheney and Frank J. Baker, Wright clients who used their engineering training in jobs with public utilities.

In the early twenties Mr. and Mrs. Dell Plain decided that they wanted to have a house designed for themselves. They owned land in Hammond, Indiana, but knew very little about architects in the area, so Mrs. Dell Plain went to Chicago early one morning to make inquiries. After talking to several people, she discovered that Howard Van Doren Shaw was a leading residential architect, and was able to arrange an appointment that same day. Given the nature of Shaw's practice at that time, their needs were rather modest, but he became interested in the project, and that same evening made sketches which met with their approval. The house was subsequently built to his design at an overall cost of $82,000 including land, landscaping, and all fees and improvements. This figure was within their budget, and today Dell Plain professes the highest regard for Shaw as a professional man.

Several aspects of this narrative demand comment. In the first place, Dell Plain was not a native-born Chicagoan and not an Ivy Leaguer, but a "new man" and a technician. Without many acquaintances in Chicago, he and his wife picked Shaw on the basis of fashion and reputation. They later chose Jens Jensen as their landscape architect in almost exactly the same way. Second, it was Mrs. Dell Plain who took the lead in the building project from the beginning. In this respect she typified what might be called the new female client of the nineteen twenties. The prairie houses had, for the most part, been built by couples in which the husband took an important, if not a dominant, role. We have observed this relationship with the Winslows, Gilmores, Robies, Greenes, and others. Now it appears to be considerably modified, if not reversed. With the granting of suffrage, a change has taken place in the role of women in American life and in the planning and design of domestic architecture.

There is additional evidence to confirm this analysis. The prairie architects who continued to practice in the Midwest, notably Barry Byrne, Richard Schmidt, and Thomas Tallmadge, were themselves conscious of their difficulties with wives and daughters. Byrne even remarked that he had a rule of thumb for determining whether or not potential clients would offer him commissions. "If the man in the household made the family decisions," writes Brooks, "Byrne felt sure of a commission, but if the wife had the final word, he knew the job was as good as lost." [5] Here again it was Shaw, not Wright, who was completely in tune with his culture. He was accustomed to dealing with couples in which the man was so completely absorbed in business affairs and active recreation that he left a large part of the program for his residence to his wife. The case of the Dell Plains is, of course, not unique. It could be repeated several times from Shaw's practice in the nineteen twenties.

What was happening to the Wright clients? In addition to the increasing feminization of American society and the sponsorship of a sophisticated eclecticism on the North Shore, they faced a variety of other problems. Consider, for example, the definition of art which came to be current in the United States at the time of the First World War. Carl Condit has written:

Art was what one was taught in the best universities, or experienced in the museums and theaters of the East, or read in the avant-garde circles that had discovered Joyce and Eliot. As far as the graphic, literary, and dramatic arts were concerned, the new taste was right, and it is understandable that what seemed to be the same view prevailed in architecture. Wealth and refinement turned to architects like Charles Follen McKim, educated, literate, at home in the salons of Europe; they certainly did not look to Sullivan, who drank whisky straight, worried about democracy, and sounded like a radical. And after all, it was not easy to judge. McKim and his architectural and engineering associates had created a triumph in Pennsylvania Station; here were brilliant and daring feats of construction, sound planning, honorable historical precedents, the power of monumental forms. The Bayard Building was scarcely noticeable by comparison. And who would expect an aesthetic experience on Bleecker Street? [6]

By the time of America's entry into the First World War, there were, in short, many excellent reasons for middle-class clients to go to revivalist architects and very few for them to approach the remaining members of the Prairie School.

If we return to the line of analysis suggested in the first chapter, it becomes clear that in comparison with earlier waves of architectural innovation, the base of support for the Wrightian revolution was exceptionally narrow. The Gothic revolution depended on the patronage of the French crown and the great bishops of the medieval church. After Abbot Suger and his architect had demonstrated the possibilities of the ribbed vault and the pointed arch in the choir of St. Denis, the movement was picked up and carried forward by a series of great personalities, like Bishop Maurice de Sully, who began the reconstruction of Notre Dame de Paris, and Kings Philip Augustus and Louis IX, who were interested in a variety of large building projects. Given the social conditions of the time, it could hardly have had more influential sponsorship. After achieving tremendous success in France in the cathedrals of Amiens,

233

Chartres, and Rheims, the Gothic went forward to further triumphs in the outlying provinces of Europe, always with approximately the same type of client. Not until the fifteenth century in Flanders did it become a bourgeois style, and then its character changed radically.

The Renaissance was scarcely less fortunate. It received its initial sponsorship from the merchant princes of Florence, who were bankers for the reigning houses of Europe. Though the Medici may have been a bit reluctant after their initial experience with Brunelleschi, the movement received the approbation of the important Rucellai family, and Leon Battista Alberti was able to carry out a surprising number of works for this powerful clan and also to spread the gospel in Rimini, Ferrara, and Mantua. His connections with the leading courts of Italy enabled him to be an influential advocate of the new style, and his literary work was even more significant. The impact of Alberti's books on architecture can scarcely be overestimated. After 1490 or thereabouts the focus of architectural activity shifted to Rome, where a number of talented designers worked on the enormous building programs of the Popes. While these programs were interrupted by the tumultuous events of the sixteenth century, the patronage of the papacy unquestionably made the style international and canonical. Versions of it sprang up in France and Spain, and somewhat later, in England, Scandinavia, the Low Countries, and the German-speaking lands. The Georgian architecture of eighteenth-century America may, in fact, be regarded as one of the last flowerings of the Renaissance, and that style, too, had the patronage of the most influential elements in society, the wealthy merchants and planters of the Atlantic seaboard. These men constituted a true colonial aristocracy and were aptly characterized by their contemporaries as "the better sort."

The Prairie School, and Wright in particular, on the other hand, drew their support from a small, highly individualized segment of the American middle class. It existed not only in Chicago and its suburbs, but also in small towns and middle-sized cities throughout the Midwest, and as one encounters its members in the best available portraits, such as John Szarkowski's chapter on Mr. and Mrs. J. R. Wheeler in *The Idea of Louis Sullivan,* they seem almost wholly admirable. They were, however, a group which lacked almost entirely the kind of institutional organization which would have enabled them to make the Wrightian revolution a permanent part of American culture. Hence when the movement lost an important base of support, as in the women's magazines, the props were literally knocked out from under it. To a certain extent the very independence of the prairie architects' clients worked against this wave of innovation. While none were antisocial

234

individuals or misanthropists, they did not belong to anything like the network of clubs and social organizations to which the Shaw clients adhered. In a curious sense they impress one as atomistic individuals, unconnected with the most significant institutions in American life. None, for example, was really active in a political party. Only a few were truly active in church affairs. The support given by Charles E. Roberts to the building project for Unity Temple suggests what might have resulted if the case had been different. It may be that we have here another instance of what might be called the classic American failure to institutionalize reform.

These early modern clients were thus a group which was extremely vulnerable to pressures which forced them, quite unconsciously, into conformity with the new standards of taste which America adopted during the decade of the First World War. During these years they were confronted by the spectacle of a regional aristocracy, the North Shore Establishment, which had obviously endorsed an architecture radically different from that which they had espoused. In addition, a variety of other large historical forces were operating on them. The reading matter of their wives and daughters changed in tone and content, and insofar as they could perceive the newest developments in literature, art, and music, these appeared to emanate from the East. It is not surprising that they shifted ground.

If we return to an earlier metaphor, we may say that the consequence of this shift was the failure of the siege. The Prairie School architecture of 1900–1917 was essentially a regional phenomenon, with its center at Chicago. Now the men who had been besieging the city withdrew from combat. Many of them actually transferred their operations elsewhere. Wright himself spent a good part of the decade in Japan, and when he returned to the United States, did most of his building during the nineteen twenties in California. It is a suggestive fact that between the Allen house of 1917 in Wichita and the Willey house of 1934 in Minneapolis he did no building in the Midwest other than additions to his own headquarters at Taliesin. After 1917 Sullivan, the philosophical leader and most sensitive spirit of the group, built only the bank for the Wheelers at Columbus, Wisconsin, but lived on in increasing poverty and loneliness until 1924. Walter Burley Griffin, one of the most talented of Wright's young men, went to Australia in 1913 and stayed there, only to endure a similar career of heartbreak and disappointment. William Gray Purcell went to Philadelphia to enter the advertising business in 1918, and various other members of the group made similar moves. Those who stayed behind, like George Maher and William Drummond, made their peace with the new order. Of the great figures of the

Prairie School, only Jens Jensen remained in the city, and he, after all, had the advantage of working in landscape design. As a consequence of this flight Chicago, and the Midwest, had to wait almost another generation for the reappearance of a vital and meaningful building art. The siege had truly been lifted, and the defense had won the battle.

6 Footnotes

[1] Thomas E. Tallmadge, *The Western Architect,* XXV (1917), p. 27.
[2] H. Allen Brooks, "The Prairie School, The Midwest Contemporaries of Frank Lloyd Wright," *Acts of the Twentieth International Congress of the History of Art* (New York, 1964), pp. 31–32.
[3] Interview with Barry Byrne, May 22, 1966.
[4] Frank Luther Mott, "House Beautiful," unpublished ms. p. 3.
[5] Brooks, "The Prairie School," p. 31.
[6] Carl Condit, *The Chicago School of Architecture* (Chicago, 1964), p. 215.

A Note on Sources

The primary source material for this book was the series of interviews with clients, their sons, daughters, and friends, gathered by Arthur LeGacy and George Mitchell and by a number of willing students. This material was, however, supplemented by information obtained from a variety of published sources. A. N. Marquis published editions of *The Book of Chicagoans* in 1905, 1911, and 1917, and these volumes were invaluable. They were supplemented by references to the *Cyclopedia of American Biography* (New York, 1895), though it should be pointed out that this source must be used with care. Its factual data are reliable, but the entries are paid for, and interpretation is sometimes a delicate question. In the same category is *Chicago and Its Makers* by Paul Gilbert and Charles Lee Bryson, a volume of generally eulogistic profiles published in the city in 1929.

On Frank Lloyd Wright the most important publications are Henry-Russell Hitchcock, *In the Nature of Materials: the Buildings of Frank Lloyd Wright 1887–1941* (London, 1942) and Grant Manson, *Frank Lloyd Wright to 1910; the First Golden Age* (New York, 1958). Both are works of great merit, but are done in the standard art-historical manner and contain little information on clients. Frederick Gutheim's compilation of Wright's literary endeavors, *Frank Lloyd Wright on Architecture* (New York, 1941), is a convenient source of writings not easily available elsewhere. The paperback *Frank Lloyd Wright: Writings and Buildings* edited by Edgar Kaufman and Ben Raeburn (New York, 1960), contains the most authoritative list of his buildings. Wright's own *An Autobiography,* available in several editions, is an immensely valuable source, but like all such documents, must be used with caution. The omissions are sometimes as revealing as the inclusions. John Lloyd Wright's *My Father Who Is on Earth* (New York, 1946) was another book important for this study.

Norris Kelly Smith, *Frank Lloyd Wright: A Study in Architectural Content* (Englewood Cliffs, New Jersey, 1966) demands particular comment. This book is an ambitious and provocative analysis of Wright's buildings and writings in terms of the visual and philosophical imagery which they present. It is in every way a remarkable work. We differ with it, however, in certain important respects. Smith sees Wright as essentially a romantic personality in the nineteenth-century sense and establishes for him an intellectual lineage with Emerson and Rousseau. His architecture is therefore basically conservative in terms of the institutional values which it embodies. "To put it bluntly," he writes, "architecture has always been the art of the Establishment" (p. 8). This statement is undoubtedly correct in a broad sense, but in our view it is not a sufficiently accurate description of the social conditions under

which Wright worked. Smith believes that the crisis of 1909–
1910 ensued because Wright had become so successful that
his self-image as a romantic hero was endangered. We think
that it happened for a variety of complex reasons, one of which
was that he finally confronted an Establishment which did, in
fact, exist, and which rejected him. Our interpretation of his
architecture is therefore more traditional in that we believe
that it was, as most historians have hitherto held, revolutionary. Finally our use of psychological theory is quite different
from that of Smith. He deals brilliantly with the artistic personality of Wright, but he seems to assume a kind of constant
client, who accepted what was offered to him with extraordinary docility. We, on the other hand, have concentrated on the
character of the clients and attempted to show that frequently
they made real contributions to the design.

The daughters of Howard Van Doren Shaw deposited two
volumes of photographs of their father's work at the Burnham
Library of the Chicago Art Institute as well as a small quantity
of office correspondence. In addition they allowed us to consult their mother's delightful unpublished memoir, *Concerning
Howard Shaw in his Home,* and were extremely helpful with
their reminiscences. Contemporary material on Shaw is abundant, since he was one of the most widely published architects of his day. The most significant articles are: Herbert

240   Croly, "Some Recent Work of Mr. Howard Shaw," *Architectural
Record* XXII (1907) pp. 421–454, Herbert Croly and C. Mat-
lack Price, "The Recent Work of Howard Shaw," *Architectural
Record* XXXIII (1913) pp. 285–329, and "Recent Country
Houses by Howard Shaw," in the *Architectural Record* for
December 1917. To these may be added shorter magazine
pieces in *House Beautiful* (January 1916), *Country Life* (March
1916), and *The Spur* (July 1, 1918, and April 1, 1919). After
Shaw's death an entire issue of *The Western Architect* was devoted to the man and his work (September 1926), and obituaries appeared in *The Architectural Record, Pencil Points,* and
The Architectural Forum. The article on Shaw by Thomas Tallmadge in *The Dictionary of American Biography* is sound and
well informed.

Within the last decade several scholars have contributed
greatly to our knowledge of Chicago architecture in the period covered by this book. Foremost among these is Carl Condit, whose book *The Chicago School of Architecture* (Chicago,
1964) is a landmark. While Condit deals mostly with commercial building, he does pay some attention to residential work,
and his remarks on the failure of architectural nerve after
1917 are extremely persuasive. H. Allen Brooks has dealt
more extensively with domestic architecture. We are particularly indebted to his "The Prairie School, Midwest Contempo-

raries of Frank Lloyd Wright" in *Studies in Western Art* (Princeton, 1963), pp. 22–33. It is Brooks who has pointed out the significance of magazines in the story and has emphasized the role of women in the movement away from the prairie architects. Mark L. Peisch has written on the career of Walter Burley Griffin in *The Chicago School of Architecture* (New York, 1964) and has also discussed the work of Purcell and Elmslie, Hugh Drummond, and various others. Almost every number of *The Prairie School Review,* published in Park Forest, Illinois, since 1964 by W. H. Hasbrouck, contains something germane to this study. The issue for the third quarter, 1965, reprints all the correspondence and some of the drawings for Wright's Sutton House at McCook, Nebraska.

Among architectural historians of a somewhat wider scope, we would especially like to mention Wayne Andrews. His *Architecture, Ambition, and Americans* is almost alone among American works in the attention which it pays to the role of the client. No student of the subject can afford to ignore Arnold Hauser's monumental *The Social History of Art* (New York and London, 1951), but the reader should be warned that Hauser's approach is that of dialectical materialism. Furthermore he is mostly concerned with sculpture and painting. Much more significant for architecture is the unpublished master's thesis of Irving Rosow, *Modern Architecture and Social Change* (Wayne State University, 1948). For our interpretation of Abbot Suger as the key client in the history of Gothic architecture we have leaned heavily on Erwin Panofsky's superb *Abbot Suger on the Abbey Church of St. Denis and its Art Treasures* (Princeton, 1946) and on Otto G. Von Simson, *The Gothic Cathedral* (Chicago). The best work on Leon Battista Alberti is Bruno Zevis' magnificent article in the *McGraw Hill Encyclopedia of World Art* (New York, London, and Toronto, 1960). Gertrude Bing has published Giovanni Rucellai's *Zibaldone* in the *Transactions* of the Warburg Institute (London, 1960) but much remains to be done on the great clients of the Renaissance.

A similar situation exists with regard to the pioneering modern architects in Europe, who were contemporaries of Wright's and Shaw's. For Henry Van de Velde there is the excellent work of A. M. Hammacher, *Le Monde de Henry Van de Velde* (Paris, 1967). This volume throws a great deal of light on the loyal circle of men who supported Van de Velde, especially during his Weimar years. For the patrons themselves see Eberhard von Bodenhausen, *Ein Leben für Kunst und Wirtschaft* (Munich, 1955), Harry Graf von Kessler, *Gesichter und Zeiten* (Berlin, 1962), and Karl Ernst Osthaus, *Van de Velde* (Hagen, 1920). Van de Velde's own autobiography, *Geschichte meines Lebens* (ed. Hans Curjel, Munich, 1962), is also valuable. The picture of life at the court of Saxe-Weimar is particularly revealing. For the other leaders of modern architecture prior to the First World War no such record exists. Although Adolf Loos wrote a good deal, he said nothing about his clients, and they are not discussed in the most recent work on him, Ludwig Munz and Gustav Künstler, *Adolf Loos, Pioneer of Modern Architecture* (New York and Washington, 1966). We would very much like to know something about the firm of Goldman Salatsch, which commissioned the famous store on the Michaelerplatz in Vienna in 1910. The patrons of Olbrich and Wagner are likewise elusive personalities. On Josef Hoffmann's relationship with the Stoclet family, there is the fine article of Eduard F. Sekler, "The Stoclet House by Josef Hoffmann" in *Essays in the History of Architecture Presented to Rudolf Wittkower* (New York, 1967) pp. 228–244. It is a good example of the type of work which needs to be done in this field.

In addition to interviews, autobiographies and secondary sources, we have relied on a number of imaginative works in the preparation of this volume. Arthur Meeker's novel *Prairie Avenue* (New York, 1946) is excellent in its depiction of the North Shore Establishment, and his *Chicago With Love* (New York, 1955) should also be mentioned. Professor Robert Weeks of the University of Michigan kindly called my attention to the importance of Ernest Hemingway's short story "Soldier's Home," available in several collections. For the Oak Park atmosphere of 1900, Charles A. Fenton's *The Apprenticeship of Ernest Hemingway* (New York, 1954) and Leicester Hemingway's *My Brother Ernest Hemingway* (Cleveland, 1962) are especially revealing. Certain novels of Booth Tarkington, especially *The Magnificent Ambersons* and *The Midlander,* are also excellent depictions of Midwestern family life in the pre-World War I period. Tarkington's sensitivity to his physical environment in Indianapolis makes one regret that he never wrote a novel with an architect as protagonist.

Appendix

by Elizabeth M. Douvan

The Design and Techniques of the Study

In an undertaking of this kind the writer owes the reader an explanation of how the thing was done. The following brief discussion describes the design and execution of the research from which the book developed. It is intended as both clarification and provocation. By describing some of the thoughts and restrictions that led to the choice of particular groups and particular questions, we hope to clarify and support the conclusions of the book. By offering both a view of the process and a summary of the raw data, we hope to provoke in the reader additional hypotheses about the Wright clients, or architectural patronage, or both.

Our first hypothesis was that anyone who built such a radical structure as a prairie house would in some way be distinguished from the general middle-class population of the American Midwest at the turn of the century. In his initial survey of the problem Professor Eaton decided to concentrate on the Wright clients of the years 1893 to 1913. He chose 1913 as a terminal date for the study in the belief that anyone who went to Wright after this time was not going to a relatively unknown young architect but to a professional man with a national and even an international reputation. By 1914 publication of his work in professional journals and in the mass media, such as the *Ladies Home Journal* and *House Beautiful,* as well as in Berlin by the Wasmuth Verlag, had made him a major figure in the nation's cultural life. To this publicity must, of course, be added the notoriety resulting from the affair with Mrs. Cheney and the tragedy at Taliesin. Wright was well, if not always favorably, known in the public press after 1913.

The Samples

The study design called for information on all clients who employed Wright from 1893 to 1913. We were interested only in those clients who were sufficiently committed to complete their building projects. According to Kaufman and Raeburn, Frank Lloyd Wright was responsible for the design and construction of eighty-six dwellings between 1893 and 1913, not counting structures which he built for himself and his family. Of these, sixty-five were located in Illinois, eight in Wisconsin, five in New York, four in Michigan, and one each in Minnesota, Ohio, Indiana, Iowa, and Nebraska. For one client, Francis W. Little, he built two houses, and for certain others, such as Edward Waller and Charles E. Roberts, he did remodelings and alterations. In view of the importance of these clients in his career we counted them, though they did not, strictly speaking, live in Wright houses. As will be seen in the text, Waller and Roberts were indirectly responsible for Wright's execution of such major commissions as Unity Church and Midway Gardens. We concentrated, however, on domestic architecture, since it was in this area that Wright made his major innovations. Of the eighty-six clients, we were able to secure substantial information on forty. The question of their representativeness will be discussed shortly. Here we should note a second requirement implied in the study objectives: the need for a control or base-line group against which to judge the description of the Wright clients. An example may be useful to clarify this requirement. As the information about Wright's clients accumulated, it became apparent that a striking number of them were inventors and gadgeteers. When a tantalizing and compelling consistency like this appears (that is, a consistency at once meaningful and neatly suited to theoretical purposes), the historian is faced with a choice. Either he can say that the group includes a remarkable number of inventors, and indicate by thoughtful analysis how this fact makes sense in relation to the selection of Wright as an architect, or he can try to add substance to the relationship by specifying his expectations and eliminating other factors that might account for the presence of so many inventors.

He could, for example, say that the number of inventors found in this group exceeds the number one would expect to find in a group this large drawn at random from the total population, or that the early Wright clients are more inventive than those who chose some other architect or who chose Wright after he had achieved eminence. The more substantial and specified statements are comparative. They require information about some group other than the target population. What population should we use for this comparative purpose? The choice will represent some amalgam of an ideal dictated by study objectives and the limits of practicality. For Professor Eaton's study the ideal might be something like "members of the Oak Park upper-middle and upper classes of the time who built houses designed by architects other than Wright." In practice this group is not available. The historian and the sociologist part company at this point: the limits set on historical studies are much the more severe. The student of contemporary groups can approximate the ideal very closely by bringing to bear modern techniques of population sampling, but the historian is restricted to groups that have left some record, people who are accessible in the special historical sense.

The most relevant available control group appeared to be a group of people who had built conservative houses in the Chicago area at approximately the same time. By starting with a conservative architect we might define a group (that is, his

246

clients) whose members could be traced historically in the same way that the Wright clients were.

Even with this purchase on the problem, one meets complications aplenty. Wright became an international figure, the subject of voluminous writings. His client lists even for the earliest projects are readily available. But the garden variety conservative architects of his day—and they were, after all, a sizable company—sank quickly into obscurity. The conservative architect whose work was significant enough to merit recording is likely to be the man of unusual prominence who built on a grand scale. Grand homes are of interest, and radical ones may inspire publication, but no one records houses (and thereby their designers) which are both modest and ordinary.

The conventional architects for whom one could hope to obtain information are limited to those who negotiated large transactions with very wealthy clients. By definition, then, these clients are different from the Wright clients on the dimensions of wealth and prominence. The clients of Howard Van Doren Shaw were as a group wealthier and closer to the center of institutional power in Chicago than were the Wright clients. Professor Eaton's presentation makes this clear.[1]

One may ask whether the Wright clients in fact could have chosen Shaw. Were they not perhaps barred from considering Shaw by simple financial limitations? If this were true, then any conclusions about unique psychological characteristics of the Wright clients based on a contrast with Shaw's clients must still be conditioned by the reservation that perhaps social class is the crucial operating determinant.

Yet the choice of Shaw as a contrast to Wright is one with unique advantages. The two architects were both visible to the community, and through publication, to a public beyond the limits of the city. They were both active in the company of architects and knew each other professionally. Professor Eaton indicates that in two instances the clients of the two men intersect socially in a way that specifically suggests a choice between them. The Coonley brothers each employed one of them. And the group geographically and occupationally close to the university, exposed to the work of both men, chose sometimes one, sometimes the other, for their personal building projects.

Even where the choice is not so clearly drawn, it should be noted that the two groups overlap considerably on the eco-

247

[1] Even for so prominent a conservative architect as Shaw no client list as such was available. No systematic work has been done on Shaw since his death in 1926, and his office records have not been preserved. Because his work was widely published, however, it was possible to generate a list of projects.

nomic and status dimensions. Wright's clients included a number of men who could certainly have afforded Shaw houses. And although Shaw clearly had a corner on the elite market, the Swifts, Armours, and Ryersons are, after all, only a part of his clientele. His commissions include many from men who were just as mobile, just as certainly self-made, as the majority of Wright's clients.

Here, it seems, is another appropriate point of intersection: two groups of self-made men, one of which achieves success in nontechnical business management, finds expression in social affairs, and moves into upper-class social position, the other succeeding through technical competence, expressing itself through musical performance and mechanical interests, and apparently caring less about conventional status and society. The groups build houses that also express this essential difference in value orientations.

The Problem of Representation

Of the eighty-six Wright clients we were able to secure a substantial amount of information on forty. By this phrase we mean that we know a good deal of the biography of the people for whom the house was built. We usually know the man's occupation, his hobbies, the clubs to which the family belonged, the number of children they had, their religious beliefs, and their politics. In a good many of these cases we also know something about the wife's activities. For five houses we were able to find surviving clients and interview them. For an additional seventeen building projects we were able to find a son, daughter, close relative, or intimate friend who was able to give us information about the clients and their relationship to Wright. In certain respects these individuals could supply an objectivity which was impossible for the clients themselves. For the remainder of our case studies we have relied on information secured from newspaper obituaries, *The Book of Chicagoans* in its various editions, the *Cyclopedia of American Biography,* and other similar sources. We have, we believe, a fair-sized sample from the complete list of Frank Lloyd Wright's early clients.

With the help of Shaw's daughters and of contemporary publications of his work, we compiled a list of ninety-one dwellings designed and constructed by Shaw during his architectural career, 1894–1926. As with Wright, we did not count houses built for the architect's immediate family, and we counted those clients who built twice (Edward Ryerson and Finley Barrell) only once. The tally is probably fairly complete, but there are undoubtedly some omissions. Of the list of ninety-one clients we have been able to compile substantial information on fifty-two. We were able to locate four surviving clients, and we secured interviews with sons, daughters, relatives, or close friends of an additional eighteen. Because the Shaw clients were, on the whole, better known than the Wright clients, it was possible to fill out their biographies rather more thoroughly from secondary sources such as *Chicago and Its Makers* (1929) and the *Cyclopedia of American Biography.* Since these works tend to be official in tone, their interpretations must be carefully evaluated. They are, however, reliable as to occupational history, club memberships, and so on, and when carefully used, yield many rewarding insights. They may be checked against *The Book of Chicagoans,* published by A. N. Marquis. It is interesting to note that Frank Lloyd Wright is not listed in any of the first three editions of this work (1905, 1911, 1917), while Shaw obtains an entry in each.

The question immediately arises: Is there any reason to believe that the unfound clients would be significantly different from the ones we have studied, and in particular, would they differ in respect to the characteristics of crucial interest in the analysis (for example, nature of occupation, inventiveness and gadgetry, musical interests)? So far as we can see, there is no reason to think so. As a matter of fact, the fragments of evidence we do possess lead us to think that they resemble the members of the sample group. Concerning Harvey P. Sutton of McCook, Nebraska, who built a Wright house in 1905, we know that he ran the town's leading jewelry shop and that his wife was an articulate and versatile woman who was active in community affairs. We know nothing of the couple's educational background, politics, or religion. We do know, however, that he was locally famous as the director of the concert band sponsored by the Chicago, Burlington, and Quincy Railroad. Similarly, we have almost no information on Henry C. Goodrich, who built in Oak Park in 1896, except that he was the inventor of a tuck marker for sewing machines and made a fair amount of money from patents on this device.

The Shaw patrons on whom information is scanty also tend to repeat the pattern of those on whom data are substantial. Concerning William P. Sidley, who built an undated Shaw house in Winnetka, we know that he was a graduate of Williams College in 1889 who subsequently studied law at Harvard and took an LL.B. degree at the Chicago College of Law. He developed a profitable law practice and was also vice president and general counsel for Western Electric. Details of his politics, religion, and family life are not known, but we do know that he was a member of the University, Union League (president), and City Clubs, and of the Skokie Country Club. He was also president of the Chicago Y.M.C.A. James O. Hinkley was another Shaw client who attended Williams. He attended Northwestern Law School but subsequently became a successful investment broker. His club memberships included the University, Union League, Midlothian, and Chicago Golf Clubs, and he was a trustee of Chicago Charity Hospital. In cases like these the Ivy League education, occupation, club memberships, and civic activities are particularly suggestive.

In short, we think that the cases we have studied can be taken as representative of the two client groups. We have no information that indicates systematic differences between cases that could be assessed in detail and those for which detailed information was unavailable. The slight information we do have about the second group suggests that on the crucial analytic variables at least, the lost cases repeat the patterns found in our sample groups.

The Questionnaire
A schedule of questions was designed to direct personal interviews whenever a client or other informant was available for questioning, and to direct research workers in their use of historical records such as official biographies and obituaries when interviewing was not feasible. The questions fall roughly into six content categories, representing different areas of speculation about the Wright clients. The categories are:

a. Questions designed to assess social status and social background of the clients (for example, education, occupation).

b. Questions focusing on independence as a value and a preferred expression (for example, political and religious attitudes and activities).

c. Questions that allow a view of the client's desire for self-expression (for example, leisure activities).

d. Questions about the client's social life as a form of self-expression.

e. Questions about the client's family life.

f. Questions about the client's relationship with the architect and the building project itself.

The hypotheses underlying the categories are in some cases clearly implied in the categories themselves; others require brief comment and clarification.

a. Social status and social background.
On the basis of Wright's comments and other prior knowledge about the clients, we expected the Wright group to be predominantly middle- and upper-middle-class men who had managed a high degree of social mobility through personal achievement in the occupational world.

b. and c. Independence and self-expression.
The typical fate of the highly mobile individual, as we know it from fiction and social theory, involves an abandonment of independent judgment in the scramble to become identical with, and acceptable to, the high-status, dominant group to

which the mobile individual aspires. In this characteristic pattern the individual seeks not unique personal expression but status expression; he builds not a radical prairie house, but a bigger and more lavish version of the customary high-status conventional house.

The Wright clients, mobile as they were, nonetheless managed to avoid this pattern. In choosing a home—the most visible declaration of life-style most people ever make—they chose an independent, even radical statement. They were evidently more interested in personal expression than in an expression of status. We expected the same independence and desire for self-expression to appear in other significant spheres: religion, politics, and leisure activities. We expected to find poets and eccentric collectors among them. And we thought they would be, in one way or another, bourgeois bohemians—religious radicals or political progressives. Needless to say, nothing of the sort turned out to be true.

d. Social life as a form of expression.

We expected the Wright clients to maintain their independence in social life as well as in other spheres. We thought they would not center their social lives about conventional country club activities. While we thought they might be quite sociable, we expected their style to be home-centered entertainment, with friends chosen for individual qualities rather than institutional attachments. We also wanted information about friendship networks as a possible medium for the spread of Wright's work.

e. and f. Family life and the relationship to Wright and the building project.

A central interest here was the clarity of sex-role division in the family. Traditionally the home is the woman's domain, particularly home furnishing and decorating. In the conventional marriage, we expect the man to participate in structural decisions, but the wife to lead in questions of design, space requirements, and, certainly, decor. The choice of a radical design, we thought, would necessitate agreement and collaboration from both husband and wife in a way that a more conventional choice would not.

We speculated beyond the specific incident of house building and suggested that the more ambiguous (and, incidentally, more modern) sex-role division would be generalized in these marriages. We expected the wives to have an independence and voice in the family not allowed in the traditional definition of the feminine role.

The complete schedule of questions, keyed to the categories, follows:

1. How old were the clients when they built? If possible, secure ages of husband and wife. (a, f)

251

2. Did the man or the woman take the lead in the building project? Who was responsible for the furnishings? Was "Decoration" the woman's province or did the man intervene? (e, f)

3. How did they hear about Frank Lloyd Wright (or Howard Van Doren Shaw)? Who made the initial approach? (f, d, e)

4. Did the job come in within the budget? If it was over, by how much? Were the clients satisfied with the professional aspect of their architect?—that is, supervision? (f)

5. Insofar as can be ascertained, what was the relationship with the architect? Stormy or harmonious? Are the memories of the architect pleasant or nasty? (f)

6. Social aspect: Who were their three best friends? How did they make friends? Church, neighbors, work, associates of husband? Was the house conceived as a backdrop for entertaining, or was it a family-centered structure? How did they use their leisure time? Golf, tennis, country club? (d, e)

7. How did the man make his living? Doctor, lawyer, businessman? If possible, get details on professional life. (a)

8. Educational background. High School? College? Professional training? (a)

9. Did they have a stable marriage? Size of family? Any divorces? (e)

10. What was their religious affiliation? Did they take it seriously? Serve on church committees, altar guilds, and so on? (b)

11. What was their political affiliation? Republican or Democratic? Were they active in politics—that is, precinct chairman, convention delegate, and so on? Were they interested in Teddy Roosevelt? How did they vote in 1912? (b)

12. Very important—were there any oddball hobbies? Did anyone write poetry or essays? Did anyone in the family collect stamps, coins, stuffed alligators? Note any evidence of nonbourgeois behavior. (c)

The Data

Item	Wright Clients	Shaw Clients
1. Total projects	86	92
2. Sample size (total)	40	52
a. interviews	22	20
b. records	18	32
3. Occupation		
a. financial — managerial	13	29
b. real estate, insurance	4	4
c. technical — managerial	17	10

d. law	2	4
e. medicine	1	2
f. academic	1	3
g. other	2	1
4. Education		
a. Some College Education Eastern	3	20
b. Some College Education Midwestern	11	13
c. Engineering	4	3
d. Postgraduate education	3	13
5. Political affiliation Activity		
a. Republican	19	31
b. Activist	6	6
c. Backed Roosevelt	4	1
d. Voted for Wilson	1	1
e. Wife active in the suffrage movement	2	0
6. Religious affiliation		
a. Protestant—conventional	16	21
b. Protestant—Liberal	7	1
c. Catholic	0	3
d. Jewish	2	5
e. Christian Science	2	0
f. None	2	2
g. Not ascertained	11	20
7. Religious activity		
a. Active in church organization	12	2
8. Civic Affairs		
a. Art Institute	1	4
b. Other museums	0	3
c. Educational affairs	3	6
d. Charitable activities	1	4
e. Hospital boards	0	2
f. Business & professional societies	4	3
g. Other	3	4
9. Club memberships *	4.7	6.7
10. Participation in Arts *		
a. Musician	11	0
b. Painter	0	1
c. Crafts	3	0

* The figures here represent the average number of memberships for the two groups. Reliable information was available for only fourteen Wright clients but for forty-five Shaw clients. Distributions would not be as meaningful for this item as are averages. The Wright data are not very reliable in any case since they are obtained from such a small number.

11. Invention, gadgetry
    a. Inventor 11   1
    b. Engineer 4   3
    c. Photographer 2   0
12. Marriage
    a. Wife emerges as individual from information interview 14   3
13. Number of children
    a. none 4   3
    b. one 7   8
    c. two 13   14
    d. three 8   7
    e. four or more 6   14
    f. Not ascertained 2   6
14. Initial contact with Architect
    a. Same social circle 10   20
    b. Referred by friend 11   5
    c. Contact originated in nonpersonal manner (exhibits, publications, attracted by a building) 6   2
15. Age
    a. Under 30 3   1
    b. 30–34 6   4
    c. 35–39 12   10
    d. 40–44 6   9
    e. 45–54 4   13
    f. 55–64 4   7
    g. Over 65 1   2
    h. Not ascertained 4   7

Index

255

256

257

258